DATE DUE

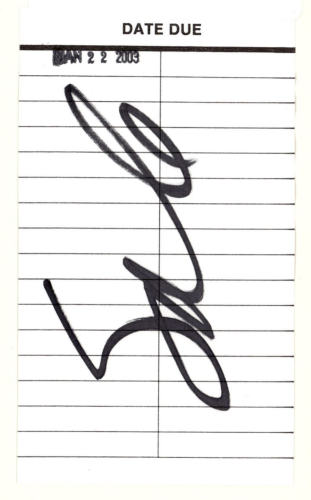

ALAN KING'S

GREAT JEWISH
JOKE BOOK

Also by the Author

Is Salami and Eggs Better Than Sex?

(Memories of a Happy Easter)

(with Mimi Sheraton)

Help, I'm a Prisoner in a Chinese Bakery

(with Hack Shurman)

Anyone Who Owns Their Own Home Deserves It

(with Kathryn Ryan)

Name Dropping—The Life and Lies of Alan King

(with Chris Chase)

ALAN KING'S
GREAT JEWISH
JOKE BOOK

Crown Publishers
New York

Published by Crown Publishers, New York, New York

Member of the Crown Publishing Group, a division of Random House, Inc.

www.randomhouse.com

CROWN is a trademark and the Crown colophon is a registered trademark of Random House, Inc.

Printed in the United States of America

Design by Leonard Henderson

Library of Congress Cataloging-in-Publication Data
King, Alan, 1927–
Alan King's great Jewish joke book / by Alan King.—1st ed.
p. cm.
1. Jewish wit and humor. I. Title: Great Jewish joke book. II. Title.
PN6231.J5 K475 2002
818'.5402—dc21   2002023724

ISBN 0-609-60924-6

10 9 8 7 6 5 4 3 2 1

First Edition

*To all the professional comedians
who told all these wonderful stories
and kept the flame alive.*

CONTENTS

FOREWORD

So, I'm reading this book, and I keep thinking of my grandma. The warmth, the sense of humor, and the big, bubbling pot of borscht. That's what this book is, a big, bubbling pot of borscht, all the ingredients melding together to give you that intoxicating, gas-giving aroma of living rooms, seders, bar mitzvahs, and nightclubs, and just plain-old sitting around the house with the relatives. It is an important collection of the best of all that. The humor that shaped me, that defines my family and friends, is all here. The wit, the knowledge, the point of view that is perfectly Jewish is here. Page after page of the good stuff, the "next three slices" the appetizer man would give my grandma after she got the nova to where she thought it should be. It's the soup from the bottom of the pot, just like the waiter at Ratner's used to give her. It's the lower half of the grapefruit after it's cut, because it's juicier, she would tell me. That's what this book is. Alan King is the perfect chef for this concoction. A master in the kitchen of komedy (K's are funny). This book will make you laugh, it will make you smile, it will make you remember those funny men and women, relatives and friends, old and young, comics and furriers, who made us laugh, and forget, for a little while, all the pain we always feel. (Hey, we're Jews, you have to throw in a little pain!) I loved the book. It made me hear my relatives again. It made me see Alan and Red and Jack Carter on *The Ed Sullivan Show* again. It's just like that borscht . . . totally delicious, and then you keep tasting it for a while. Thank you, Alan.

—*Billy Crystal*

INTRODUCTION

It is said that a Jewish joke is a joke that a Gentile won't "get," and a joke that a Jew has heard and knows how to tell it better.

But anyone who has ever laughed at a joke doesn't need to be told that Jewish humor is not only ubiquitous, it's, well, just *funnier* than most other humor. It's certainly no mere coincidence that behind most great humor is a Jewish writer. In fact, the list of famous Jewish comedians and writers is completely overwhelming. I am more than proud to be on that list.

Jewish wit is sharp, and it cuts deeply. There are many theories about why this is so. Most prominent among these theories is that Jewish wit is a defense mechanism. That would certainly be understandable, given that Jews are among the most persecuted people in the history of the world. Humor helps get us all through life's difficulties, so if its origins are in suffering and survivalism, that's no mystery.

I've probably heard—and told—some of the jokes in this book a thousand times; more than a few are older than I am. Others were actually new to me. But I couldn't think of a good Jewish joke that isn't in this collection.

Some of the jokes are the stuff of folklore. In fact, this book could be viewed as part of an oral history of Jewish Americans. And I'd be shocked if you could get through the book without calling at least five people to read them a joke or two.

Throughout this book you will encounter a great deal of sheer mercurial wit, which has characterized the Jewish people for as long as anyone can remember. This is partly because one of the most highly prized characteristics in all of Jewish culture is intelligence, and the better part of wit is intelligence.

Enjoy!

—*Alan King*

ALAN KING'S
GREAT JEWISH
JOKE BOOK

THE JEWISH PSYCHE

The jokes in this chapter create a kind of overview of some significant preoccupations that characterize "the Jewish psyche." We get the worrywart, the hypochondriac, the money-grubbing miser, the intractable negotiater.... Some would say certain of these refer to the stereotypical, or "stage" Jew. But objectively speaking, the only crime in humor is an unfunny joke. Let's face it: It's difficult enough to be funny without worrying about what is going to offend whom.

If you stop and think about it, nearly all great humor is at the expense of someone or something. So take off your "politically correct" hat and have a great time!

* * *

Jewish telegram: "Begin worrying. Details to follow."

The Law of Conservation of Jewish Behavior Among Reform Jews

This Extremely Reform Jewish principle, adapted from Newtonian physics, provides that "for each and every Jewish act, there is an equal and opposite non-Jewish act."

Thus, if you do a small kindness for someone less fortunate than you, you are permitted to eat a shrimp cocktail.

If you visit a sick person in the hospital, you may spend the Sabbath at a restricted country club.

When two Jews argue they will have at least three opinions.

Three men were staggering through the desert.

The first, a Frenchman, exclaimed, "I'm so hot, I'm so thirsty, I must have wine!"

The second, an Italian, shouted, "I am very hot, I am very thirsty, I must have wine!"

The third, a Jew, cried out, "I am so hot, I am so thirsty, I must have . . . diabetes!"

Yaakov was walking on the beach and noticed an old lamp. He picked it up and rubbed it. A genie suddenly came out of the bottle and said, "Gee thanks, Yaakov! I'm the Jewish Genie! I've been locked in this bottle for over two hundred years! Because you have released me I'll grant you three wishes. However, I have to warn you that what you get, your lawyer will get double."

Yaakov thought for a while, then said, "For my first wish, I'd like one hundred million gold coins."

The genie said, "Okay, but remember, your lawyer will get two hundred million gold coins."

Yaakov said, "That's okay."

Then the genie granted Yaakov's wish. Poof! There, right in front of him, was a hundred million gold coins.

Then Yaakov said, "For my second wish, I would like a fifty-acre ranch on the French Riviera with a thirty-room home overlooking the bluffs into the ocean."

The genie said, "Okay, but remember, your lawyer will be next door with twice the acreage and in a house twice as large and he likes to party twenty-four hours a day."

Yaakov said, "I think I can live with that."

Then the genie granted Yaakov's wish. Poof! There he was, on the French Riviera, and next door was his attorney just as the genie had said.

So the genie said, "For your third wish you'd better think long and hard."

After thinking it over, Yaakov said, "Could you please scare me half to death?"

A flood worse than the days of Noah was foretold. Nothing could be done to prevent it; in just three days, the waters would wipe out the entire world.

The leader of Buddhism appeared on TV and pleaded with

everyone to become a Buddhist; that way, they will at least find salvation in heaven.

The pope went on TV with a similar message: "It is still not too late to accept Jesus as your savior," he said.

The chief rabbi of Israel took a slightly different approach: "We have three days," he said, "to learn how to live under water."

A resident pediatrican was making his rounds in the ward, trailed by six interns. "Sickle cell anemia may be found in black children, especially if their parents come from the Caribbean. Tay-Sachs disease occurs in adult Jews, of course, but Jewish children are more easily identified by one fact. Can anyone tell me what that is?"

"Certainly," one intern chimed in. "Heartburn."

Three hunters were out on safari—an American, a Brit, and an Israeli. They were captured by cannibals who started preparing their cooking pots.

The cannibal chief told the hunters they could have one last wish.

"What's your last request?" he asked the American.

"I'd like a steak," he replied.

So the cannibals killed a zebra and served the American his steak.

"What do you want?" the cannibal chief asked the Brit.

"I'd like to have a smoke on my pipe," which they permitted him to do.

Then the chief asked the Israeli: "What's your last wish?"

"I want you to kick my rear end."

"Be serious," said the head cannibal.

"C'mon, you promised, whatever I wanted," said the Israeli.

"Oh, all right," sighed the chief, who delivered the requested kick. Whereupon, the Israeli pulled out a gun and shot the chief and a few other cannibals while the rest ran away.

The American and Brit were furious.

"Why didn't you do that in the first place, so we wouldn't have had to go through all this?" they demanded.

The Israeli replied: "What? Are you mad? The UN would have condemned me as the aggressor."

A visitor came to Israel and saw the Western Wall. Not being too well versed in religious aspects, he inquired of another tourist about the significance of the wall. The other tourist explained, "This is a sacred wall. If you pray to it, God may hear you."

The visitor walked close to the wall and started to pray. "Dear Lord," he said, "bring sunshine and warmth to this beautiful land."

A commanding voice answered, "I will, my son."

The visitor said, "Bring prosperity to this land."

"I will, my son."

"Let Jews and Arabs live together in peace, dear Lord."

The voice answered, "You're talking to a wall."

Three men were standing in line to get into heaven one day. Apparently it had been a pretty busy day, though, so Malach

Gavriel (Angel Gabriel) had to tell the first one, "Heaven's getting pretty close to full today, and I've been asked to admit only people who have had particularly horrible deaths. So what's your story?"

The first man replies, "Well, for a while I've suspected my wife has been cheating on me, so today I came home early and tried to catch her red-handed. As I came into my twenty-fifth-floor apartment, I could tell something was wrong, but all my searching around didn't reveal where this other guy could have been hiding. Finally, I went out to the balcony, and sure enough, there was this man hanging off the railing, twenty-five stories above the ground! By now I was really mad, so I started beating on him and kicking him, but wouldn't you know it, he wouldn't fall off. So finally I went back into my apartment and got a hammer and starting hammering on his fingers. Of course, he couldn't stand that for long, so he let go and fell, but even after twenty-five stories, he fell into the bushes, stunned but okay. I couldn't stand it anymore, so I ran into the kitchen, grabbed the fridge, and threw it over the edge where it landed on him, killing him instantly. But all the stress and anger got to me, and I had a heart attack and died there on the balcony."

"That sounds like a pretty bad day to me, all right," said Malach Gavriel, and let the man right in.

The second man approaches and Malach Gavriel explains to him about Heaven being full, and asks for his story. "It's been a very strange day. You see, I live on the twenty-sixth floor of my apartment building, and every morning I do my exercises out on my balcony. Well, this morning I must have slipped or some-thing, because I fell over the edge. But I got lucky, and caught the railing of the balcony on the floor below me. I knew I couldn't hang on for very long, when suddenly this man burst out onto the balcony. I thought for sure I was saved, when he started beating on me and kicking me. I held on the best I could until he ran into the apartment and grabbed a hammer and started pounding on my hands. Finally I just let go, but again I got lucky and fell into the bushes below, stunned but all right. Just when I was thinking I was going to be okay, this refrigerator comes falling out of the sky and crushes me instantly, and now I'm here."

Once again, Malach Gavriel had to concede that that sounded like a pretty horrible death, and into heaven the man went.

The third man came to the front of the line, and again the whole process was repeated. Malach Gavriel explained that heaven was full and asked for his story.

"Picture this," says the third man. "I'm hiding naked inside a refrigerator. . . . "

When a severe hurricane blew across the Caribbean, it wasn't long before the expensive yacht was swamped by high waves, sinking without a trace. There were only two survivors: the boat's owner, Dr. Eskinfeld, and its steward, Benny, who managed to swim to a nearby island.

After reaching the deserted strip of land, the steward was weeping, certain that they would never be found. The other man was quite calm, relaxing against a tree.

"Dr. Eskinfeld, Dr. Eskinfeld, how can you be so calm?" cried Benny. "We're going to die on this lonely island. We'll never be found here."

"Calm down and listen to what I have to say, Benny," replied the doctor. "Five years ago I gave the United Way $500,000. And I gave another $500,000 to the United Jewish Appeal. I donated the same amounts four years ago. And three years ago, since I did very well in the stock market, I contributed $750,000 to each. Last year business was good, so the two charities each got a million dollars."

"So what?" Benny shouted.

"Well, it's time for their annual fund drives, and I know they're going to find me," smiled Dr. Eskinfeld.

Here are six classic Jewish insults and curses:

"May you inherit a hotel and die in every room."

"May you grow like an onion, with your head in the ground."

"May your bones be broken as often as the Ten Commandments."

"May you have a son named after you soon."

"May the souls of all of King Solomon's mothers-in-law inhabit you."

"May God mistake you for your worst enemy and give you all the curses you wished on him."

Abraham the Patriarch had some of the most famous arguments with God to be found in the entire Bible. Among the most memorable was the disagreement over the fate of Sodom and

Gomorrah. There was a lesser-known discussion between God and Abraham. It had to do with the nature of the Covenant and the ultimate reward of the Jewish People. It is said that Abraham asked God for clarification. The discussion ended something like this:

Abraham: "Okay, God, let me see if I've got this straight. The Arabs get all the oil, and we get to cut the ends of our penises off?"

A religious man lived a good life and always felt God had treated him well. One day the water of a nearby river crested above the banks and a flood began. While all his neighbors evacuated, he stood fast and told them he wasn't worried, that God would provide.

As the water reached his roof, a man in a raft came by and told him to hop on. He said no, that God would provide.

With the water now halfway up his roof a man in a rowboat came and implored that the man come with him. He refused saying God would provide.

Finally a helicopter came and dropped a rope as the waters rose even higher. He still stood fast at the top of his roof, insisting that God would provide. The helicopter flew away, and soon the rising water carried the man to his death.

At the gates of heaven the man asked God why he did not save him.

God replied, "What do you mean? I sent you two boats and a helicopter!"

Jewish Grammar Rules

1. Phrase statements as questions. Instead of telling Ida she looks gorgeous, ask her, "How stunning do you have to look?"

2. Instead of answering questions with a statement, answer with another question. When someone asks how you feel, answer, "How should I feel?"

3. Whenever possible, end questions with "or what?" This allows the other person to interject another question: "Has she grown up, or what?" "Can you remember when she was just a baby, or what?" (About now, a spontaneous rendition of "Sunrise, Sunset" should be expected.)

4. Begin questions with "What?" Example: "What, my cooking's not good enough for you?"

5. Drop last word in sentence (which is typically a direct or indirect object): "What, do you want to get killed going alone? Harry will go with" (drop "you").

6. Move subject to end of sentences: "Is *she* getting heavy, that Esther?"

7. Use "that" as a modifier to infer contempt: "Is Esther still dating that Norman fellow?"

8. Use "lovely" to describe actions taken by someone else that the listener should have done, too: "We got a lovely note from the Goldmans for hosting the seder." (Translation: "What, you didn't eat and drink at my seder? You slob, you didn't send a thank-you note!")

A Russian asked an Englishman, "Why isn't there any anti-Semitism in your country?"

The Englishman replied, "Because we don't think Jews are smarter than we are."

A Jewish man and a Chinese man were conversing. The Jewish man commented upon what a wise people the Chinese are.

"Yes," replied the Chinese. "Our culture is over four thousand years old. But you Jews are a very wise people, too."

The Jewish man replied, "Yes, our culture is over five thousand years old."

The Chinese man was incredulous. "That's impossible," he replied. "Where did your people eat for a thousand years?"

An American tourist in Tel Aviv was visiting the impressive Mann Auditorium to take in a concert by the Israel Philharmonic. He particularly admired the unique architecture and the modern decor throughout the building. Finally, he turned to his escort and asked if the building was named for Thomas Mann, the world-famous author.

"No," his friend said, "it's named for Fredric Mann, from Philadelphia."

"Really? I never heard of him. What did he write?"

"A check."

Jewish Vocabulary

Just as the Eskimos have twenty-seven words for snow, Jews have thirty-one words for neurotic.

It is very difficult to know when to call someone *meshugge,
farmisht, furdrehet, hot nisht ein kaup,* or *vaist nisht vus vus ehr
reht.* . . . Here are a few words to get you started.

1. "*Sch—*" as a prefix to anything, suggests disapproval: "Cadillac,
   schmadillac, you're suddenly too good for the Lincoln?"
2. Learning to pronounce "*sch*" properly is the first step in speaking
   Hebonics like a real Jew. Nothing makes us giggle harder than the
   sound of Gentiles saying, "It's not raining, just spritzing." It's the
   same "ssshhh" sound as the prompt to be quiet.
3. *Schmuck*—Most commonly used as "jerk," but can also be used as
   a "sucker," as in, "Why am I always the *schmuck* who gets left with
   the check?"
4. *Schmoe*—See *schmuck.*
5. *Schmata*—Rag (ugly dress), as in, "Why does she wear those
   schmatas, that Esther?"
6. *Schmaltz*—Literally means chicken fat, but when used in conversation it's sappy or corny. "The movie was OK, but why such a
   schmaltzy ending?"

Jewish Bumper Stickers

Jesus saves. Moses invests.
If it tastes good, it's probably not kosher.
Why spoil a good meal with a big tip?
No meal is complete without leftovers.
What business is a yenta in? Yours.

Prozac is like chicken soup: It doesn't cure anything, but it
makes you feel better.

It is said that most really great violinists of the last century are and were Jews. There are, however, very few Jews among the greatest pianists. Why do you suppose this is the case?

Have you ever tried to make your escape with a piano?

Morris called his son in New York and said, "Benny, I have something to tell you. But I don't want to discuss it. I'm merely telling you because you're my oldest child, and I thought you ought to know. I've made up my mind, I'm divorcing Mama."

The son was shocked, and asked his father to tell him what happened.

"I don't want to get into it. My mind is made up."

"But Dad, you can't decide to divorce Mama just like that after fifty-four years together. What happened?"

"It's too painful to talk about it. I only called because you're my son, and I thought you should know. I really don't want to get into it any more than this. You can call your sister and tell her. It will spare me the pain."

"But where's Mama? Can I talk to her?"

"No, I don't want you to say anything to her about it. I haven't told her yet. Believe me it hasn't been easy. I've agonized over it for several days, and I've finally come to a decision. I have an appointment with the lawyer the day after tomorrow."

"Dad, don't do anything rash. I'm going to take the next flight down. Promise me that you won't do anything until I get there."

"Well, all right, I promise. Next week is Passover. I'll hold off seeing the lawyer until after the seder. Call your sister in New

Jersey and break the news to her. I just can't bear to talk about it anymore."

A half hour later Morris received a call from his daughter, who told him that she and her brother had been able to get airline tickets and that they and the children will be arriving in Florida in two days. "Benny told me that you don't want to talk about it on the telephone, but promise me that you won't do anything until we both get there."

Morris promised.

After hanging up with his daughter, Morris turned to his wife and says, "Well, it worked this time, but what are we going to do next Yom Tov to get them to come down?"

So You Think You Know Jews . . .

If you are an aspiring Jew—or even if you've been Jewish all your life—and you're marrying into a Jewish family, there are certain things you'll need to know in order to survive. Take this quiz to see if you've learned enough in this life to function in your new Jewish family:

1. There are no Jews living in:
   a. sin
   b. El Paso
   c. trailer parks

2. The cleaning lady in a Jewish household is expected to:
   a. do windows
   b. make latkes
   c. attend all bar mitzvahs and weddings

3. To make a good pet for a Jewish child, an animal must be:
   a. gentle
   b. housebroken
   c. stuffed

4. Jews spend their vacations:
   a. sight-seeing
   b. sunbathing
   c. discussing where they spent their last vacation and where they'll spend the next

5. If there's a hairdresser in your immediate family, you are:
   a. up on the newest styles
   b. entitled to free haircuts
   c. not Jewish

6. Wilderness means:
   a. no running water
   b. no electricity
   c. no hot and sour soup

7. The most popular outdoor sport among Jews is:

   a. jogging

   b. tennis

   c. howling over the neighbors' lawn ornaments

8. Jews never drive:

   a. unsafely

   b. on Saturdays

   c. eighteen-wheelers

9. A truly unsuitable gift for a Jewish person is:

   a. Easter lilies

   b. a crucifix

   c. a Zippo lighter

10. A Jewish skydiver is:

    a. careful

    b. insured

    c. an apparition

11. No Jewish person in history has ever been known to:

    a. become a prostitute

    b. deface a synagogue

    c. remove the back of a TV set

12. Jews never sing:

    a. off-key

    b. "Nel Blu di Pinto di Blu"

    c. around a piano bar

13. Jews are ambivalent about:

   a. vegetarianism

   b. Jesse Jackson

   c. absolutely nothing

Scoring: Take 1 point for each "a" answer, 2 for each "b," 3 for each "c."

39–41: Mazel Tov! You know a lot about Jews. Either you've studied your loved one's family carefully, out of desire for true closeness and your respect for their traditions, or you're from either Florida or New York. They'll adore you.

29–38: You're not quite there yet, but don't panic. Just remember to do everything louder, longer, and with a lot more butter than you're used to.

17–28: Sorry. Better study harder. Or consider getting a divorce and buying a Denny's franchise.

Great Jewish Proverbs

A fool is his own informer.

Hope may give a man strength, but not sense.

A schlemiel lands on his back and bruises his nose.

Spare us what we can learn to endure.

A heavy purse makes a light heart.

Love is blind, but jealousy sees too much.

A dead man is mourned seven days, a fool his lifetime.

Some people may be compared to new shoes: The cheaper they are, the louder they squeak.

You can't force anyone to love you or to lend you money.

No man suffers for another's sins—he has enough of his own.

Your health comes first—you can always hang yourself later.

Money is round, so it rolls away.

Love your neighbor, even when he plays the trombone.

One good deed has many claimants.

Blind is he who thinks he sees everything.

God is an honest payer, but a very slow one.

If you want to get a reputation as a wise man, agree with everybody.

Rejoice not at your enemy's fall, but don't pick him up either.

The girl who can't dance says the band can't play.

We have far greater compassion for someone else's misfortune than the pleasure we take in his good fortune.

Life is the cheapest bargain—you get it for nothing.

The best part about telling the truth is that you don't have to remember what you said.

It is easier to spot faults in others than virtues in oneself.

God loves the poor and helps the rich.

If you lie on the ground, you can't fall.

A good friend you get for nothing; an enemy you've got to buy.

The heaviest thing in the world is an empty pocket.

May God protect you from goyish *hands and from* Yiddishe *tongues.*

Understanding is something we are certain the other fellow hasn't got.

God will provide. If only God would provide until He provides!

Treat me like a rabbi and watch me like a thief.

If you begin to think of death, you're no longer sure of your life.

If I dealt in candles, the sun wouldn't set.

OBSERVANCE

*A*rguments about observance among Jews, even among Jews of the same sect, are even more animated than arguments about the best way to make noodle kugel. The way that Orthodox or Traditional Jews feel about Reform Jews is no secret. But even Reform Jews have serious differences when it comes to observance. All aspects of Jewish life are examined through the prismatic lens of observance, and there's plenty of room for humor when something that's taken so seriously somehow leaves so much room for difference of opinion.

* * *

When an Orthodox Jew talks to God, he says "Riboynoy-sheloylom" (Master of the World).

When a Conservative Jew is in touch with God, he calls Him "Avinu Malkeinu" (Our Father, Our King).

A Reform Jew addresses God as "Oh Lord, Thou art One."

A Reconstructionist says "To whom it may concern."

*   *   *

A non-Jew is curious: Is having sex on the Sabbath a sin? He wasn't sure whether sex was considered work or play. So first he asked a priest.

After consulting the Bible, the priest told him, "My son, after an exhaustive search I am positive sex is work and is not permitted on Sundays."

The man thought: "What does a priest know about sex?"

So he went to a minister, a married man and a father, for the answer. He queried the minister and received the same reply: Sex is work and not for Sunday.

Not pleased with the reply, he sought the ultimate authority: a man of thousands of years tradition and knowledge—a rabbi. The rabbi pondered the question and stated, "Sex is definitely play."

The man asked, "Rabbi, how can you be so sure when all the other religious men told me that sex is work?"

The rabbi replied, "If sex were work, my wife would have the maid do it."

A worried woman asked her rabbi, "Am I permitted to ride in an airplane on *Shabbos*?"

"Yes," the rabbi replied, "as long as your seat belt remains fastened. Then it is considered that you are wearing the plane."

Traditional vs. Reform Observance

Traditional: Farm animal must be killed by ritual slaughterer using a sharply honed knife that must not have a single nick on its blade.

Reform: Farm animal must be told that it has the right to an attorney.

Traditional: Will not combine meat with milk.

Reform: Will not combine meat with chocolate milk.

Traditional: One set of dishes for meat, another set for dairy.

Reform: One set of dishes exclusively for cheeseburgers.

Traditional: Hire *Shabbos goy* to perform religiously prohibited tasks.

Reform: Hire Orthodox Jew to perform religiously required tasks.

Traditional: Try to concentrate on prayers, achieve sense of being in the presence of the divine.

Reform: Try to figure out when to stand up, when to sit down, and what page everyone is on.

Traditional: Women required to sit in synagogue balcony, apart from men.

Reform: Women and men sit together, davening suggestively.

Traditional: Strong disapproval of women rabbis.

Reform: Strong disapproval of topless women rabbis.

An old Jewish man was dying in the hospital. His family—wife, children, grandchildren—came to see him, but only one visitor was allowed in the room at a time.

Grandson Ben went in first. "Hello, Grampa Moishe. Can I do something for you?"

"Yes," said Grampa Moishe, "go tell Gramma Sadie I want some of her chopped liver."

Ben went out and told Gramma Sadie, who said, "Go tell Grampa Moishe he can't have any chopped liver. It would kill him."

Ben went back in and reported that Grampa Moishe said, "You tell Gramma Sadie I want the chopped liver. I'm dying anyway and it won't make any difference."

Ben went and told Gramma Sadie, who said, "Go tell Grampa Moishe he can't have any. The chopped liver is for the shiva."

A dental hygienist always encouraged her patients to floss. During one cleaning, the dentist asked his patient if he were "flossing religiously."

"Well," the man admitted, "I floss more often than I go to synagogue."

A Short Summary of *Every* Jewish Holiday:

"They tried to kill us. We won. Let's eat."

*　　*　　*

In a slalom skiing race, the skier must pass through about twenty "gates" as rapidly as possible. It came to pass that Israel had the fastest slalom skier in the world, and the country had great expectations for an Olympic gold medal.

The day of the final came, and the crowd waited in anticipation.

The French champion sped down the course in 38 seconds. The Swiss was clocked at 38.7 seconds, the German at 37.8 seconds, and the Italian at 38.1 seconds.

Then came the turn of the Israeli. The crowd waited, and waited . . . *six minutes!* "What happened to you?" screamed his trainer when the Israeli finally arrived.

The exhausted Israeli replied: "Who fixed a mezuzah to each gate?"

Why is it so important for the groom at a Jewish wedding to stomp on a wineglass?

Because it's the last time he'll put his foot down.

Rules for Jewish Living

1. Never take a front-row seat at a bris.
2. If you can't say something nice, say it in Yiddish.
3. The High Holidays have nothing to do with marijuana.
4. And what's wrong with dry turkey?
5. A good kugel sinks in mercury.

6. Pork is forbidden, but a pig in a blanket makes a nice hors d'oeuvre.

7. Always whisper the names of diseases.

8. One mitzvah can change the world; two will just make you tired.

9. Never leave a restaurant empty-handed.

10. The important Jewish holidays are the ones on which alternate-side-of-the-street parking is suspended.

11. A bad matzoh ball makes a good paperweight.

12. Without Jewish mothers, who would need therapy?

13. According to Jewish dietary law, pork and shellfish may be eaten only in Chinese restaurants.

14. If you are going to whisper at the movies, make sure it's loud enough for everyone else to hear.

15. No meal is complete without leftovers.

16. If you have to ask the price, you can't afford it. But if you can, make sure you tell everybody what you paid.

17. The only thing more important than a good education is a good parking spot at the mall.

18. It's not who you know, but who you know who's had breast implants.

19. After the destruction of the Second Temple, God created Loehmann's.

20. WASPs leave and never say good-bye; Jews say good-bye and never leave.

21. Israel is the land of milk and honey; Florida is the land of milk of magnesia.

22. If you don't eat, it will kill me.

23. Anything worth saying is worth repeating a thousand times.

24. Next year in Jerusalem. The year after, how about a nice cruise?

25. Spring ahead, fall back, winter in Miami.

26. Laugh now, but one day you'll be driving a big Cadillac and eating dinner at four in the afternoon.

27. There comes a time in every man's life when he must stand up and tell his mother that he is an adult. This usually happens at around age forty-five.

The following announcements were actually found in shul newsletters and bulletins:

Remember in prayer the many who are sick of our congregation.

Don't let worry kill you. Let your synagogue help.

For those of you who have children and don't know it, we have a nursery downstairs.

We are pleased to announce the birth of David Weiss, the sin of Rabbi and Mrs. Abe Weiss.

The ladies of Hadassah have cast-off clothing of every kind and they may be seen in the basement on Tuesdays.

Weight Watchers will meet at 7 P.M. at the JCC. Please use the large double door at the side entrance.

The rabbi is on vacation. Massages can be given to his secretary.

Please join us as we show our support for Amy and Rob, who are preparing for the girth of their first child.

If you enjoy sinning, the choir is looking for you!

*   *   *

It is reported that the following part of the Book of Genesis was discovered in the Dead Sea Scrolls. If authentic, it would shed light on the question, "Where do pets come from?"

And Adam said, "Lord, when I was in the garden, you walked with me every day. Now I do not see you anymore. I am lonesome here and it is difficult for me to remember how much you love me."

And God said, "No problem! I will create a companion for you that will be with you forever and who will be a reflection of my love for you, so that you will know I love you, even when you cannot see me. Regardless of how selfish and childish and unlovable you may be, this new companion will accept you as you are and will love you as I do, in spite of yourself."

And God created a new animal to be a companion for Adam. And it was a good animal. And God was pleased.

And the new animal was pleased to be with Adam and he wagged his tail. And Adam said, "But Lord, I have already named all the animals in the Kingdom and all the good names are taken and I cannot think of a name for this new animal."

And God said, "No problem! Because I have created this new animal to be a reflection of my love for you, his name will be a reflection of my own name, and you will call him 'Dog.'"

And Dog lived with Adam and was a companion to him and loved him. And Adam was comforted. And God was pleased. And Dog was content and wagged his tail.

After a while it came to pass that Adam's guardian angel came to the Lord and said, "Lord, Adam has become filled with pride. He struts and preens like a peacock and he believes he is worthy of adoration. Dog has indeed taught him that he is loved, but no one has taught him humility."

And the Lord said, "No problem! I will create for him a companion who will be with him forever and who will see him as he is. The companion will remind him of his limitations, so he will know that he is not always worthy of adoration."

And God created Cat to be a companion to Adam. And Cat would not obey Adam. And when Adam gazed into Cat's eyes, he was reminded that he was not the supreme being. And Adam learned humility.

And God was pleased. And Adam was greatly improved.

And Cat did not care one way or the other.

An Englishman in New York stopped at a window in the middle of which stood one lone clock.

The Englishman went inside.

"Hello!" he called.

From behind a curtain stepped a bearded man in a skullcap.

"Would you please inspect this watch?" The Englishman worked at the strap. "Tell me whether it needs—"

"Why are you asking me?" asked the bearded one.

"Aren't you a jeweler?"

"No. I'm a *mohel*."

"A what?"

"A *mohel*. I perform circumcisions."

"Good Lord!" exclaimed the Englishman. "But why do you have a clock in your window?!"

"Mister," sighed the *mohel*, "what would *you* put in the window?"

An elderly rabbi retired from his duties in the congregation and he decided to fulfill his lifelong fantasy—to taste pork. He went to a hotel in the Catskills in the off-season (not his usual hotel, mind you), entered the empty dining hall, and chose a table far in the corner. The waiter arrived, and the rabbi ordered roast suckling pig.

As the rabbi waited, struggling with his conscience, a family from his congregation walked in! They immediately saw the rabbi, of course, and since no one should eat alone, they joined him. The rabbi began to sweat. Finally, the waiter arrives with a huge domed platter. He lifted the lid to reveal—what else?—a whole roast suckling pig, complete with an apple in its mouth.

"This place is amazing!" cried the rabbi. "You order a baked apple, and look what you get!"

A newly observant house painter, wondering how he could correct his previous misdeeds, was meeting with his rabbi during the Days of Awe.

"Rebbe, I've done awful things as a painter. I've done sloppy jobs, used inferior-quality paints and lied about it, I cut my paints with turpentine, and cut corners. How can I make up for these evil deeds that I've committed in a previous life?"

The Rebbe thought for a while, looked at the painter, and then pronounced: "Repaint, Repaint, and thin no more."

Top Ten Reasons to Like Hanukkah

10. No roof damage from reindeer

9. Never a silent night when you're among your Jewish loved ones

8. If someone screws up on their gift, there are seven more days to correct it

7. Betting Hanukkah gelt (the chocolate coins) on candle races

6. You can use your fireplace

5. Naked spin-the-dreidel games

4. Cool waxy buildup on the menorah

3. No awkward explanations of virgin birth

2. Cheer optional

1. No Irving Berlin songs

A priest and a rabbi were discussing the pros and cons of their particular religions, and inevitably the discussion turned to repentance.

The rabbi explained Yom Kippur, the solemn Day of Atonement, a day of fasting and penitence, while the priest told him all about Lent and its forty days of self-denial and absolution from sins.

After the discussion ended, the rabbi went home to tell his wife about the conversation.

She began laughing uproariously. The rabbi says, "What's so funny, dear?"

She replied, "Forty days of Lent, one day of Yom Kippur! So even when it comes to sin, the goyim pay retail!"

What's the difference between a bris and a get (a Jewish divorce)?
In a get, you get rid of the whole schmuck!

Rabbi Friedman, quite Orthodox, couldn't believe his eyes: There in the restaurant, clearly visible through the large window, was the president of his congregation eating a big bowl of creamed clam chowder. As the rabbi watched in horror, the main dish, jumbo shrimp wrapped in bacon, was set down next. Oblivious to the rabbi's disgusted visage, the president ate his way through his dinner.

As he left the restaurant, the rabbi accosted him: "You . . . you of all people, leader of the congregation, supposed to be setting an example, how could you eat such *trayf*?!"

The president replied: "You saw me eat the soup? And the shrimp?"

"Yes, and yes" came the reply.

"Then there's no problem: I ate my food under rabbinical supervision!"

What is the technical term for an uncircumcised Jew who is over eight days old?
A girl.

BAR/BAS MITZVAHS

A *young man's or woman's rite of adulthood is a solemn occa-sion that has exploded over the years into an excuse for a nearly bacchanalian festivity. Parents' efforts to outdo other mem-bers of their congregation alone make excellent, if obvious, fodder for jokes. But as we shall see, grandmothers, mice, and even bees can be brought into the bar/bas mitzvah fray in the name of humor.*

* * *

A bar mitzvah is the day when a Jewish boy suddenly realizes that he is more likely to own a professional sports team than to play for one.

Glenn Teitlebaum's bar mitzvah was to be held at Water's Edge in Long Island City, one of the fanciest party spaces in the tristate area. The room upstairs and the pier outside were lav-ishly decorated with cascades of flowers. The buffet table was overflowing with over seventy hot and cold delicacies, and ice sculptures spewing bright pink punch were at either end of the long table.

Glenn's aunt and uncle were among the last to arrive. They looked the place over and immediately became annoyed by the ostentatiousness of it all. They were civil rights workers, and it really bothered them to see such flagrant waste. But their nephew's bar mitzvah was required attendance, or Mama Teitlebaum would never forgive them.

As they walked to one of the three open bars for a drink, Glenn's mother greeted them warmly. "Isn't it a beautiful affair?" she asked breathlessly. Pointing to a life-size sculpture of the guest of honor made entirely of chopped liver, she inquired, "What do you think of the gorgeous statue of my Glenn?"

Uncle Harry could bear it no longer. That stupid statue alone cost more than he made in six months. In a voice fairly dripping with sarcasm, he snarled, "Why, I've never seen anything like it. Who did it? Lipschitz or Epstein?"

"Lipschitz, of course, darling," bragged the proud mother. "Epstein works only in halvah!"

One Labor Day weekend, two bees were buzzing around what's left of a rosebush.

"How was your summer?" asked bee number one.

"Not too good," replied bee number two. "Lotta rain, lotta cold. Not enough flowers, not enough pollen."

The first bee said, "Hey, why don't you go down the corner and hang a left? There's a bar mitzvah going on. Plenty of flowers and fruit."

Bee two buzzed, "Thanks!" and took off for the bar mitzvah.

An hour later, the bees ran into each other again. "So, how was the bar mitzvah?" asked the first bee.

"Great!" replied the second.

The first bee peered at his pal and asked, "What's that on your head?"

"A yarmulke," he answered. "I didn't want them to think I was a wasp."

A rich man wanted the most spectacular bar mitzvah ever held for his son. After months of pondering the alternatives, the father finally decided to arrange to rent a space shuttle from NASA and take his family and the rabbi into space. That created a lot of attention, and when the shuttle returned home, the press was there to find out how everything had gone.

The first person off the shuttle was the grandmother. The reporters asked, "How was the service?"

Grandma answered, "Okay."

"How was the boy's speech?"

"Okay."

"How was the food?"

"Okay."

"Everything was just okay? You don't seem to have liked it very much? What was wrong?"

"There was no atmosphere!"

*　　*　　*

A priest, minister, and rabbi were having lunch. The priest was complaining about a problem he was having with mice in his church.

The minister noted that he had had the same problem and called professional exterminators to get rid of the mice, but they had no success.

The rabbi said he once had the same problem, but no longer.

"How did you get rid of them?" asked the priest and the minister.

"Simple," said the rabbi, "I put some cheese on top of the dais, and when the mice came to eat the cheese, I bar mitzvah'd them. That was the last time I ever saw them!"

JEWISH WOMEN AND THE JEWISH AMERICAN PRINCESS

Jewish women—and particularly Jewish American princesses— are the most prominent cultural stereotypes in all of Jewish American humor. Jewish mothers get a chapter of their own, of course, and Jewish American princesses, or JAPs, here get a sub-chapter of their own. After all, almost everyone who has ever heard a joke has heard a JAP joke, and JAP characters are all over television sitcoms and movies. Herein is a selection of the best JAP jokes we could find. But we'll begin with the funniest jokes about Jewish women in general.

*　　*　　*

The Harvard School of Medicine did a study of why Jewish women like Chinese food so much. The study revealed that this is due to the fact that Wonton spelled backwards is Not Now.

Where does a Jewish husband hide money from his wife?
Under the vacuum cleaner.

*   *   *

When the doctor called Mrs. Liebenbaum to tell her that her check came back, she replied, "So did my arthritis."

The rabbi was carefully explaining to a group of eight-year-old students the story of Elijah the Prophet and the false prophets of Baal. He explained how Elijah built the altar, put wood upon it, cut the steer in pieces, and laid it upon the altar. And then Elijah commanded the people of God to fill four barrels of water and pour it over the altar. He had them do this four times.

"Now," the rabbi said to the class, "can anyone tell me why the Lord would have Elijah pour water over the steer on the altar?"

A little girl in the back of the room raised her hand with great confidence. "To make the gravy," came her enthusiastic reply.

What's the difference between a Catholic wife and a Jewish wife?
The Catholic wife tells her husband to buy Viagra.
The Jewish wife tells her husband to buy Pfizer.

Close to drowning, Benny Cohen was pulled out of the ocean by a lifeguard. His wife ran over sobbing, "Benny! Benny, what happened?!"

"Madam, please don't get hysterical," said the lifeguard, "I'm just going to give your husband some artificial respiration and he'll be fine."

"What?" Mrs. Cohen yelled. "My Benny gets either real respiration or nothing."

Ruth and Golda, two Jewish women, were walking along the street. Ruth told Golda, "My son, Irving, is finally getting married. He tells me he is engaged to a wonderful girl, but . . . he thinks she may have a disease called herpes."

Golda said to Ruth, "Do you have any idea what this herpes is, and can he catch it?"

Ruth answered, "No, but I am just so thrilled to hear about Irving's engagement. It's past time he's settled. As far as the herpes goes . . . who knows?"

"Well," Golda said, "I have a very fine medical dictionary at home. I'll look it up and call you."

So Golda went home, looked it up, and, quite relieved, called Ruth. "Ruth, I found it. Not to worry! It says . . . 'herpes is a disease of the gentiles!'"

A man asked his wife, "What would you most like for your birthday?"

She answered, "I'd love to be ten again."

So on the morning of her birthday, he got her up bright and early and off they went to a huge nearby amusement park. What a day! He put her on every ride in the park: the Death Slide, The Screaming Loop, the Rotor, the Wall of Fear, six or seven roller coasters—everything there was!

She staggered out of the amusement park five hours later, her head reeling and her stomach upside down. Right into McDonald's they went, and her husband ordered a Double Big Mac for her along with extra fries and a refreshing strawberry shake. Then off to a movie. He picked the latest Star Wars epic, and hot dogs, popcorn, Pepsi Cola, and a big bag of M&Ms.

Finally she wobbled home with her husband and collapsed on the bed.

He leaned over her lovingly and asked, "Well, dear, what was it like being ten again?"

One eye opens and she groans, "Schmuck, I meant dress size!"

A new forestry graduate received his first five-year posting way out in the middle of a huge forest with no people around for miles.

Much to his surprise, included in the survival gear they give him was a recipe for matzoh balls.

When he asked why a matzoh ball recipe was included, he was told, "Sometime, a few years down the road, when the solitude *really* starts to get to you, you'll pull out this matzoh ball recipe and start to mix it together. And then—*bam*! Within five minutes you'll have half a dozen Jewish women hovering over you telling you what you're doing wrong!"

A Jewish man locked himself out of his car on a scaldingly hot summer day. He looked through the garbage and found a wire hanger. He went back to his car to try to open the lock.

He shoved the wire through the slightly open window with his wife telling him, "Harold, move it more to the right . . . more to the left . . . Higher! Lower!"

Finally his wife said, "What's taking you so long?"

To which Harold replied, "It's easy for you to say, sitting inside an air-conditioned car!"

One day in the Garden of Eden, Eve calls out to God, "Lord, I have a problem!"

"What's the problem, Eve?"

"Lord, I know you've created me and have provided this beautiful garden and all of these wonderful animals, and that hilarious comedy snake, but I'm just not happy."

"Why is that, Eve?" came the reply from above.

"Lord, I'm lonely. And I'm sick to death of apples."

"Well, Eve, in that case, I have a solution. I shall create a man for you."

"What's a 'man,' Lord?"

"This man will be a flawed creature, with aggressive tendencies, an enormous ego, and an inability to empathize or listen to you properly. All in all, he'll give you a hard time. But he'll be bigger and faster and more muscular than you. He'll be really good at fighting and kicking a ball about and hunting fleet-footed ruminants, and not altogether bad in the sack."

"Sounds great," says Eve, with an ironically raised eyebrow.

"Yeah, well. He's better than a poke in the eye with a burnt stick. But you can have him on one condition."

"What's that, Lord?"

"You'll have to let him believe that I made him first."

A woman could never get her husband to do anything around the house. He would come home from work, sit in front of the TV, eat dinner, and sit some more. He never did those little household repairs that most husbands take care of. This considerably frustrated the woman.

One day the toilet got stopped up. When her husband got home, she said sweetly, "Honey, the toilet is clogged. Would you look at it?"

Her husband snarled, "What do I look like? The tidy-bowl man?" and sat down on the sofa.

The next day, the garbage disposal wouldn't work. When her husband got home, she said, very nicely, "Honey, the disposal won't work. Would you try to fix it for me?"

Once again, he growled, "What do I look like? Mr. Plumber?"

The next day, the washing machine was on the blink. When her husband got home, she steeled her courage and said, "Honey, the washer isn't running. Would you check on it?"

And again she was met by a snarl, "What do I look like? The Maytag repairman?"

Finally, she had had enough. The next morning, the woman called three repairmen to fix the toilet, the garbage disposal, and the washer. When her husband got home, she said, "Honey, I had the repairmen out today."

He frowned. "Well, how much is that going to cost?"

"Well, honey, they all said I could pay them by baking them a cake or having sex with them."

"Well, what kind of cakes did you bake them?" he asked.

She smiled. "What do I look like? Betty Crocker?"

Leah and Shifrah were old friends. They had both been married to their husbands for a long time. But Shifrah became upset one day because she thought her husband didn't find her attractive anymore.

"As I get older he doesn't bother to look at me!" Shifrah cried.

"I'm so sorry for you," Leah said. "It's funny, with my husband it's the opposite. As I get older he tells me I get more beautiful every day."

"Yes," said Shifrah, "but your husband's an antiques dealer!"

Thanks to a theatrical agent and good friend, Mr. and Mrs. Greenberg finally got tickets to see *The Producers* on Broadway. This was the most sold-out show of the year, especially after it won thirteen Tony Awards. Scalpers were retiring on this one.

They'd actually lucked into front-row seats. But they noticed that in the row behind them, there was an empty seat. When intermission came and no one had sat in that seat, Mrs. Greenberg turned to the woman sitting next to it and asks, "Pardon me, but this is such a sold-out show, and in such demand. We were wondering why that seat is empty."

The woman said, "That's my late husband's seat."

Mrs. Greenberg was horrified and apologized for being so insensitive.

But a few minutes later, she turned around again.

"Without meaning to be rude or anything . . . surely you must have a friend or a relative who would have wanted to come and see this show?"

The woman nodded, but explained, "They're all at the funeral."

Several women were visiting elderly Mrs. Diamond, who was very ill. After a while, they rose to leave, and told her, "Esther, we will keep you in our prayers."

"Just wash the dishes in the kitchen," the ailing woman said. "I can do my own praying."

Sometime after Sidney died, his widow, Tillie, was finally able to speak about what a thoughtful and wonderful man her late husband had been.

"Sidney thought of everything," she told them. "Just before he died, Sidney called me to his bedside and he handed me three envelopes. 'Tillie,' he told me, 'I have put all my last wishes in these three envelopes. After I am dead, please open them and do exactly as I have instructed. Then I can rest in peace.'"

"What was in the envelopes?" her friends asked.

"The first envelope contained $5,000 with a note, 'Please use this money to buy a nice casket.' So I bought a beautiful mahogany casket for him.

"The second envelope contained $10,000 with a note, 'Please use this for a nice funeral.' I made Sidney a very dignified funeral and bought all his very favorite foods for when we began shiva."

"And the third envelope?" asked her friends.

"The third envelope contained $25,000 with a note, 'Please use this to buy a nice stone.'" Tillie held up her hand and pointed to her ring finger, on which there was a ten-carat diamond ring. "So," said Tillie, "you like my stone?"

Four women in their late fifties were playing mah-jongg one day and one woman stopped playing and blurted out, "I have to tell you all something. I'm a kleptomaniac! But I want you to know, I've *never* taken anything from any of you."

The next woman said, "Well, as long as we're being honest, I feel I have to tell you three: I'm a nymphomaniac! But I have my own circle of people, and I've never hit on any of your family members or friends."

The third woman admitted, "Well, I'm a lesbian, but you have no worries. I've never been attracted to any of you."

The fourth woman jumped up and cried, "Well, I'm a yenta and I have to go make some phone calls!"

Mrs. Goldberg went to the doctor for a checkup.

When he was finished, the doctor said to Mrs. Goldberg, "I have to tell you that you have a fissure in your uterus, and if you ever have a baby it would be a miracle."

She went home and told her husband: "You vouldn't belief it. I vent to the doctah and he told me, 'You haf a fish in your uterus and if you haf a baby it vill be a mackerel!'"

When Morty Blumenthal reached the age of seventy-five, he suddenly began chasing young women one-third his age.

A well-meaning neighbor brought this behavior to the attention of his wife. "What are you going to do about it?" she asked.

"Nothing! Who cares?" said Mrs. Blumenthal. "Let him chase girls! Dogs chase cars, but when they catch them, they can't drive!"

A man was walking down the street in Tampa when a beautiful woman appeared out of nowhere right in front of him, completely nude and with green skin.

Stunned, the man spoke to her. "Excuse me, but I'm amazed that you just popped out of thin air. How did you do that?"

"Oh," the woman explained, "I'm from Andromeda, in what you call Outer Space."

"Andromeda?" said the man. "I can't believe it. Do all the women on Andromeda have green skin like you?"

"Yes, everyone is green on Andromeda," replied the woman.

The man continued to stare and speak. "Excuse me for asking, but I can't help but notice that you have twelve toes on each foot. Here on Earth we have five toes on each foot. Do all Andromedans have twelve toes on each foot?"

"Yes," replied the woman. "Everyone on Andromeda has twelve toes on each foot."

"And forgive me for saying, but it's hard not to notice that you have three breasts. Earthwomen have only two breasts. Do all Andromedans have three breasts?"

"Yes," replied the woman, "everyone on Andromeda has three breasts."

"Please, may I ask you just one more question?" the man asked.

"Sure," replied the woman.

"I also can't help but notice that on each of your hands you have seven fingers and on each finger you have a large diamond. Here on Earth diamonds are very rare and valuable. Do all Andromedan women have diamonds on their fingers?"

"Well . . . ," the woman answered, "not the goyim."

It must be admitted that sometimes women are overly suspicious of their husbands. It's a tendency that goes right back to the very beginning.

When Adam stayed out very late for a few nights, Eve became upset.

"You're running around with other women," she charged.

"You're being unreasonable," Adam responded. "You're the only woman on Earth."

The quarrel continued until Adam fell asleep, only to be awakened by someone poking him in the chest. It was Eve.

"What do you think you're doing?" Adam demanded.

"Counting your ribs," replied Eve.

Top Ten Reasons Why God Created Eve

10. God worried that Adam would always be lost in the garden, because he knew men would never ask directions.

9. God knew that Adam would one day need someone to hand him the TV remote, because men don't want to see what's on television, they want to see *what else* is on television.

8. God knew that Adam would never buy a new fig leaf when the seat wore out and therefore would need Eve to get one for him.

7. God knew that Adam would never make a doctor's appointment for himself.

6. God knew that Adam would never remember which night was garbage night.

5. God knew that if the world was to be populated there would have to be someone to bear them, because men would never be able to handle it.

4. As "Keeper of the Garden," Adam would never remember where he put his tools.

3. The scripture account of creation indicates that Adam needed someone to blame his troubles on when God caught him hiding in the garden.

2. As the Bible says, "It is not good for man to be alone." He only ends up getting himself in trouble.

1. When God finished the creation of Adam, he stepped back, scratched his head and said, "I can do better than that."

Once upon a time in a faraway land there lived a king who had a Jewish adviser. The king relied so much on the wisdom of his

Jewish adviser that one day he decided to elevate him to head adviser. After it was announced, the other advisers objected. After all, it was bad enough to have to sit in counsel with a Jew, but to allow one to "Lord it over them" was just too much to bear.

Being a compassionate ruler, the king agreed with them, and ordered the Jew to convert. What could the Jew do? One had to obey the king, and so he did.

As soon as the act was done, the Jew felt great remorse for his terrible decision. As days became weeks, his remorse turned to despondency, and as months passed, his mental depression took its toll on his physical health. He gradually became weaker and weaker.

Finally he could stand it no longer. His mind was made up. He burst in on the king and cried, "I was born a Jew and a Jew I must die. Do what you want with me, but I can no longer deny my faith."

The king was very surprised. He had no idea the Jew felt so strongly about it. "Well, if that's how you feel," he said, "then the other advisers will just have to learn to live with it. Your counsel is much too important to me to do without. Go and be a Jew again," he said.

The Jew was utterly elated. He hurried home to tell the good news to his family. He actually felt the strength surge back into his body as he ran. Finally, he burst into the house and called out to his wife.

"Rivkah, Rivkah! We can be Jews again, we can be Jews again!"

His wife glared back at him angrily and said, "You couldn't wait until after Passover?"

*   *   *

A woman visited her rabbi and told him, "Rabbi, I have a problem. I have two female talking parrots, but they only know how to say one thing."

"What do they say?" the rabbi inquired.

"They only know how to say, 'Hi, we're prostitutes. Want to have some fun?'"

"That's terrible!" the rabbi exclaimed. "But I have a solution to your problem. Bring your two female parrots over to my house and I will put them with my two male talking parrots whom I taught to pray and read Hebrew. My parrots will teach your parrots to stop saying that terrible phrase and your female parrots will learn to praise and worship."

"Thank you so much, rabbi!" the woman replied.

The next day the woman brought her female parrots to the rabbi's house. His two male parrots are wearing tiny yarmulkes and praying in their cage. The lady put her two female parrots in with the male parrots and the female parrots said, "Hi, we're prostitutes, want to have some fun?"

One male parrot looked over at the other male parrot and exclaimed, "Put away the siddurs! Our prayers have been answered!"

A middle-aged woman suffered a heart attack and was taken to the hospital.

While on the operating table she had a near-death experience.

During it, she saw God and asked him if this was the end of her life.

God said no and explained that she had another thirty to forty years to live.

Upon her recovery, she decided to just stay in the hospital and have a face lift, liposuction, breast enlargement, tummy tuck—the works. She even had someone come in and change her hair color. She figured since she had another thirty to forty years she might as well make the most of it.

But when she walked out the hospital after the last operation, she was killed by an ambulance speeding up to the emergency room.

She arrived before God and said, "I thought you said I had another thirty to forty years."

God replied, "I didn't recognize you."

What's the difference between Jewish women and Catholic women?

Catholic women have fake jewelry and real orgasms.

Sarah came home from her date, rather sad. She told her mother, "David wants to marry me."

Her mother says, "David's such a good boy. Why such a sad face on my *bubeleh*?"

"Mama, David is an atheist. He doesn't even believe there's a hell."

Her mother says, "*Bubeleh,* marry him! Between the two of us, we can make him a believer."

*   *   *

Anna, not the brightest woman in the congregation, went to see her rabbi. He could see she was angry. Actually, she was in quite a state. She told him she wanted to divorce her husband.

"Whatever for? What's the matter?" he asked.

"I have a strong suspicion he's not the father of our youngest child!"

Two women were sitting next to each other on an airplane. One is in her twenties, the other in her fifties.

The younger woman says to the elder, "Excuse me, but I couldn't help notice that beautiful diamond ring you're wearing. It's just incredible."

The older woman replies, "Thank you. This is the famous Plotnick Diamond, you know."

"The Plotnick Diamond? I've never heard of it."

"Oh yes, it's very famous. The Plotnick Diamond."

"Well," says the younger woman, "it really is beautiful. I would give anything to have a diamond like that."

"*No!* Don't say that!" exclaims the older woman. "Believe me, darling, you do not want to own this diamond!"

"But why not?"

"Because there is a terrible curse attached to this diamond, that's why."

"A curse?" the younger woman asks.

"Yes, a curse. The terrible Plotnick Curse. A curse so awful and horrible that I wouldn't wish it on my worst enemy!"

"Well, what kind of curse could possibly be so terrible?"

To which the older woman replies, lowering her voice slightly, "Mister Plotnick."

Mrs. Rosen invited several couples over for dinner. When everyone had gathered at the table, she turned to her six-year-old daughter, Sarah, and said, "Would you like to say the blessing, dear?"

Sarah said, "I don't know what to say."

My wife said, "Just say what you hear Mommy say."

Her daughter bowed her head and said: "Oh Lord, why on earth did I invite all these people to dinner?"

JAPS

Have you seen the newest Jewish American princess horror movie?
It's called "Debbie Does Dishes."

What's a Jewish American princess's favorite position?
Facing Bloomingdale's.

What is a Jewish American princess's favorite wine?
"I wanna go to Palm Springs!"

How do JAPs prepare their children for supper?
Put them in the car.

How many JAPs does it take to change a lightbulb?
Two. One to open the Diet Pepsi, and the other to call Daddy.

You know you're a JAP if . . .
Neiman Marcus is number two on your cellular's speed dial.
You've had diamond studs soldered into your earlobes.
You actually know the difference between carats and karats.
You hire an architect to design your new house in Alpha World.
Your dog owns more clothing and toys than your neighbor's children.
The only thing you know how to make for dinner is reservations.
*You decorate a Hanukkah bush and insist upon eight gifts to get you
in the mood!*
*If your daddy buys you a Jeep Grand Cherokee and you ask him to take
it back because it's simply the wrong color, then you may be a JAP.*
*If it costs you $100 to get a haircut and an extra $150 to get it col-
ored, then you might be a JAP.*
*If you don't talk to people because they don't own anything made by
Tommy Hilfiger, then there is a possibility that you may just be a JAP.*
*If you only wear black clothes when you go out and your closet has
been designated as an official Black Hole, then there is a chance
that you might be a JAP.*
*If you are rich, Jewish, and from Long Island, Miami Beach, or Bev-
erly Hills, then people might think you're a JAP.*
*If you keep a taxi on call to whisk you from one class to another, then
most people would agree that you're a JAP.*
*If you carry your mirror, credit cards, and cellular phone in a minia-
ture Gucci backpack, then some people might consider you a JAP.*

If you have an absolutely perfect nose that doesn't quite match your
face, then there is a remote possibility that you may be a JAP.

Naomi went to Atlantic City for the first time ever and decided to play roulette. She asked someone at the table the best way to pick a number. He suggested putting her money on her age. So she put ten chips on number 28. When number 34 came up, she fainted.

At the conclusion of the physical exam, a doctor summoned his patient into his office with a grave look on his face. "I hate to be the one to break it to you, Fred," he said, "but I'm afraid I'd only be able to give you six more months to live."

"Oh, my gosh," gasped Fred, turning white. When the news had sunk in he said, "Listen, Doc, you've known me a long time. Do you have any suggestions as to how I could make the most of my remaining months?"

"You've been a bachelor all your life, Fred," the doctor replied. "You might think about taking a wife. After all, you're going to need someone to look after you during the final stages of your illness."

"That's a good point, Doc," mused Fred. "And with only six months to live I'd better make the most of my time."

"May I make one more suggestion?" asked the doctor.

Fred nodded. "Of course, doctor."

"Marry a Jewish girl."

"A Jewish girl, how come?"

"It'll seem longer."

JEWISH BOYS AND MEN

*T*he place of Jewish men in American society has always been complicated, in part because the nature of Jewish men is itself so complex. With a heritage that so strongly stresses intellectual stamina and social expectations that include strict adherence to the work ethic, it's no wonder that the stereotypical Jewish man is often a nebbish—timid, meek, and ineffectual. But keeping body and soul and family and community together is no laughing matter. Or is it?

*   *   *

A Jewish boy comes home from school and tells his mother he's been given a part in the school play. "Wonderful. What part is it?"

The boy says, "I play the part of the Jewish husband."

The mother scowls and says, "Go back and tell the teacher you want a speaking part."

David, a little Orthodox Jewish boy, was having trouble at school. In fact, he was kicked out of the school. His parents had no idea what to do, so they consulted a social worker. She said, "For the good of the child, he must go to a public school. Clearly he needs more freedom to express himself."

The parents are in shock: Our boy in a public school?

In the end, they sent David to public school. On only the second day, this third grader was expelled. The parents returned to the social worker and asked her what to do now. "You see," the social worker told them, "David really needs more structure, and it was my mistake. You must send him to a military academy."

"What? Our son in the army?"

But soon they sent him to the academy, and after two days he was court-martialed and expelled. Not knowing what to do, they went back to the social worker, who told them, "There is only one alternative, and that's a Catholic school."

The parents were in shock. "Our child David, going to *them*?"

But they had little choice, so in the end they sent him to Catholic school. David became the perfect student. In fact, at the end of the year the seniors asked him to speak to the graduating class.

His parents had to ask David: "First our school, then the public school, then the military school—nothing worked. Why, all of a sudden, with the Catholics, did you become the model student?"

David looked at his father and said, "Dad, the first day the Mother Superior sat me down in the chair and pointed to the giant crucifix above the chalkboard and said, 'See that? That's the last Jewish boy who misbehaved here!'"

*   *   *

A rabbi said to a precocious six-year-old boy, "So, your mother says your prayers for you each night? Very commendable. What does she say?"

The little boy replied, "Thank God he's in bed!"

A young Jewish boy began attending public school in a small town. The teacher of the one-room school decided to use her position to try to influence the new student. She asked the class, "Who was the greatest man who ever lived?"

A girl raised her hand and says, "I think George Washington was the greatest man who ever lived, because he is the Father of our country."

The teacher replied, "Well, that's a good answer, but that's not the answer I'm looking for."

Another young student raised his hand and said, "I think Abraham Lincoln was the greatest man who lived, because he freed the slaves and helped end the civil war."

"Well, that's another good answer, but that is not the one I was looking for."

Then the new Jewish boy raised his hand and announced, "I think Jesus Christ was the greatest man who ever lived."

The teacher's mouth dropped open in astonishment. "Yes!" she exclaimed. "That's the answer I was looking for."

She then brought him up to the front of the classroom and gave him a lollipop.

Later, during recess, another Jewish boy approached him as he was licking his lollipop. "Why did you say Jesus Christ was the greatest man who ever lived?" he asked

The boy stopped licking his lollipop and replied, "I know it's Moses, and *you* know it's Moses, but business is business."

A rabbi asked a six-year-old boy what his favorite Bible story was.

"I guess the one about Noah and the ark, where they floated around on the water for forty days and forty nights," replied the boy.

"That was a good story," said the rabbi, "and, with all that water, I bet they had a good time fishing, don't you think?"

The boy thought for a moment, then replied, "I don't think so . . . they only had two worms."

A father was reading Bible stories to his young son.

He read, "The man named Lot was warned to take his wife and flee out of the city and never look back. But his wife did look back and so was turned to salt."

His son asked, "What happened to the flea?"

A sixteen-year-old boy had just received his driver's license. He asked his father, who was a rabbi, if they could discuss the use of his car. His father told him, "I'll make a deal with you. You bring home good grades, study your Bible a little, and get your hair cut, and then we'll discuss the use of the car."

After about a month the boy again asked his father if he could use the car. His father replied, "Son, I've been very proud of you. You have brought your grades up, you've studied your Bible diligently, but you didn't get your hair cut!"

The young man replied, "Well, Dad, I've been thinking about that. You know, Samson had long hair, Moses had long hair, Noah had long hair—"

His father interrupted: "Yes, and they also *walked* everywhere they went!"

There once were two young brothers, eight and ten years old, who were exceedingly mischievous. Whenever anything went wrong in the neighborhood, it turned out that they had had a hand in it. Their parents were at their wits' end trying to control them.

One day they heard about a rabbi in town who worked with delinquent boys. The mother suggested to her husband that she ask the rabbi to talk with the boys and he agreed.

So the mother went to the rabbi and made her request. He agreed, but said he wanted to see the younger boy first and alone. So the mother sent the younger to the rabbi.

The rabbi sat the boy down and sat across from him behind his enormous, impressive desk. For about five minutes they just sat and stared at each other. Finally, the rabbi pointed his forefinger at the boy and asked, "Young man, where is God?"

The boy looked under the desk, in the corners of the room, all around, then said nothing.

Again, louder, the rabbi pointed at the boy and asked, "Where is God?" Again, the boy looked all around but said nothing.

A third time, in a louder, firmer voice, the rabbi leaned far across the desk and put his forefinger almost to the boy's nose, and demanded, "Young man, I ask you, where is God?"

The boy panicked and ran all the way home. Finding his older brother, he dragged him upstairs to their room and into the closet, where they usually plotted their mischief. He finally said, "We're in bi-i-i-i-i-i-i-g trouble."

The older boy asked, "What do you mean, *big* trouble?"

His brother replied, "I'm tellin' ya', we're in *big* trouble. God is missing and they think we did it!"

Little Shmuel came home from school and, as was the family custom, told his father what he had learned that day.

"Papa, the teacher says we have all been born to help others."

"She's quite right," said the father.

"But Papa, why were the others born?"

The following is—allegedly—a real job application that was submitted at a fast-food restaurant.

NAME: Shlomo Gold

DESIRED POSITION: Whatever's available. If I was in a position to be picky, I wouldn't be applying here.

DESIRED SALARY: $185,000 a year plus stock options and a severance package. If that's not possible, make an offer.

EDUCATION: Yes

LAST POSITION HELD: Target for middle-management hostility

SALARY: Not enough!

HOURS AVAILABLE TO WORK: Any

PREFERRED HOURS: 1:30–3:30 P.M., Monday, Tuesday, and Thursday.

MAY WE CONTACT YOUR CURRENT EMPLOYER?: If I had one, would I be here?

DO YOU HAVE A CAR?: . . . that runs? No!

HAVE YOU RECEIVED ANY SPECIAL AWARDS OR RECOGNITION?: I received a letter notifying me that I may be a winner of the Publishers Clearinghouse Sweepstakes.

DO YOU SMOKE?: Only when set on fire

WHAT WOULD YOU LIKE TO BE DOING IN FIVE YEARS?: Living in the Bahamas with a fabulously wealthy supermodel who thinks I'm the greatest thing since sliced bread

DO YOU CERTIFY THAT THE ABOVE IS TRUE AND COMPLETE TO THE BEST OF YOUR KNOWLEDGE? Of course

SIGN: Scorpio with Libra rising

Abe wandered into the local tavern and saw his friend Moishe sitting at the bar. He puts his hand to his heart and shouted:

"*Oy vay,* Moishe! I'm so sorry to hear about your shop burning down."

Moishe spun around quickly and said, "Shhhh . . . it's tomorrow!"

A team of archaeologists was excavating in Israel when they came upon a cave. Drawn across the wall of the cave were the following symbols, in this order of appearance: a women, a donkey, a shovel, a fish, and the Star of David.

They decided that this was a unique find and that the writings were at least three thousand years old. They chipped out the piece of stone wall and had it brought to the museum, where archaeologists from all over the world came to study the ancient symbols. They held a huge meeting after months of conferences to discuss the meaning of the markings.

The president of the society stood up and pointed at the first drawing and said: "This looks like a woman. We can judge that the race was family-oriented and held women in high esteem. You can also tell that they were intelligent, as the next symbol resembles a donkey, so, they were smart enough to have animals to help them till the soil.

"The next drawing looks like a shovel of some sort, which means they even had tools to help them. Even further proof of their high intelligence was in the fish, which means that if a famine had hit the earth, whereby the food didn't grow, they would take to the sea for food.

"The last symbol appears to be the Star of David, which means they were evidently Hebrews."

The audience applauded enthusiastically.

Suddenly a little old man stood up in the back of the room and said: "Idiots! Hebrews read from right to left. It says: 'Holy Mackerel, Dig the Ass on that Woman!'"

"I'm so upset," Sol Hershberg told his rabbi. "I took my son-in-law into my clothing business, and yesterday I caught him kissing one of the models!"

"Have a little patience!" advised the rabbi. "After all, guys will be guys. So he kissed one of the models, it's not so terrible."

"But you don't understand," said Hershberg. "I make men's clothes!"

Old Mr. Hirsch went to the doctor for a checkup.

After extensive tests the doctor came to him and said, "I'm afraid I have some bad news for you, Mr. Hirsch. You only have six months to live."

Mr. Hirsch was dumbstruck. After a few moments he replied, "That's terrible, doctor! But I have to admit to you that I can't afford to pay your bill."

"Okay," said the doctor, "I'll give you a year to live."

There was once a cunning man who went to his rich neighbor and asked to borrow a silver spoon. The rich man gave it to him.

A few days later, the borrower returned the spoon and with it a small spoon.

"What's that for?" the rich man asked. "I lent you only one spoon."

"Your spoon," the borrower replied, "gave birth to this little spoon, so I have brought you back both mother and child, because both belong to you."

Although what the man said sounded foolish, the rich man, who was greedy, accepted both spoons.

A while later the cunning man again went to his rich neighbor and asked this time to borrow a large silver goblet. And the rich man lent him a silver goblet.

Several days later the borrower returned the goblet and with it a little goblet.

"Your goblet," he told him, "gave birth to this little goblet. I'm returning them because both belong to you."

After a while the cunning man paid a third visit to his rich neighbor and said to him: "Would you mind lending me your gold watch?"

"With pleasure!" answered the rich neighbor, thinking to himself that it would be returned to him together with a small watch. So he gave him his beautiful gold watch, which was set with diamonds.

One day passed, then another, and still another, but the borrower failed to show up with the watch. The rich man became impatient and went to the house of his neighbor to make inquiry.

"What happened to my watch?" he asked.

The cunning borrower heaved a deep sigh. "I am sorry to tell you that your watch is dead! I had to get rid of it."

"Dead? What do you mean dead?" cried the rich man angrily. "How can a watch die?"

"If a spoon can bear little spoons," answered the cunning man, "and if a goblet can bear little goblets, why should it surprise you that a watch can die?"

Jacob found himself in dire straits. His business had suddenly gone under and he was in serious financial trouble. He was so desperate that he decided to ask God for help.

He went into the synagogue and began to pray: "God, please help me, I've lost my business and if I don't get some money, I'm going to lose my house as well; please let me win the lottery."

The lottery night came and somebody else won it.

Jacob returned to the synagogue. "God, please let me win the lottery, I've lost my business, my house, and I'm going to lose my car as well."

Lottery night came and went and Jacob still had no luck.

Back to the synagogue he went. "My God, why have you forsaken me? I've lost my business, my house, my car, and my wife and children are starving. I don't often ask you for help and I have always been a good servant to you. Why won't you just let me win the lottery this one time so I can get my life back in order?"

Suddenly there was a blinding flash of light as the heavens opened and Jacob was confronted by the voice of God Himself: *"Jacob, meet me halfway on this one and buy a #@% ticket!"*

Morty and Sam, not terribly religious men, were walking their dogs by the temple on Saturday morning.

Morty suggested, "Let's go in. I hear they have chopped liver at the Oneg Shabbat every Saturday."

Sam said, "They will never let us in with the dogs."

"Just follow my lead," said Morty, and into the temple he went.

The shammes stopped him and said, "No dogs are allowed in temple."

Morty said, "It's my Seeing Eye dog!"

The shammes said, "Okay, then go ahead."

Sam followed.

Again the shammes said, "No dogs are allowed in temple."

Sam said, "This is my Seeing Eye dog!"

The shammes asked Abe, "This is your Seeing Eye dog? A chihuahua?"

Sam looked startled and said, "Is *that* what they gave me?"

Jerome was almost twenty-nine years old. His friends had all already gotten married and Jerome just dated and dated.

Finally a friend asked him, "What's the matter? Are you looking for the perfect woman? Are you that particular? Can't you find anyone who suits you?"

"No, not at all," Jerome replied. "I meet many nice girls, but as soon as I bring them home to meet my parents, my mother doesn't like them. So I keep on looking!"

"Listen," his friend suggests, "why don't you find a girl who's just like your dear old mother?"

Many weeks passed and again Jerome and his friend got together.

"So, Jerome, did you find the perfect girl yet? One who's just like your mother?"

Jerome shrugged his shoulders, "Yes, I found one just like Mom. My mother loved her. They became fast friends."

"So do I owe you a mazel tov? Are you and this girl engaged yet?"

"I'm afraid not. My father can't stand her!"

*　　*　　*

A middle-aged Jewish man took his wife out to dinner to celebrate her fortieth birthday. He asked her, "So what would you like, Julie? A Jaguar? A sable coat? A diamond necklace?"

She said, "Bernie, I want a divorce."

He said, "Gee, I wasn't planning on spending that much."

A young man asked a rich old man how he'd made his money.

The old man fingered his cardigan sweater and replied, "Well, son, it was 1932, the depth of the Great Depression. I was down to my last nickel. I invested that nickel in an apple. I spent the entire day polishing the apple and, at the end of the day, I sold the apple for ten cents.

"The next morning, I invested those ten cents in two apples. I spent the entire day polishing them and sold them at 5:00 P.M. for twenty cents. I continued this system for a month, by the end of which I'd accumulated a small fortune of $1.37.

"Then my wife's father died and left us two million dollars."

A man boarded an airplane and took his seat. As he settled in, he glanced up and saw the most beautiful woman boarding the plane. He soon realized she was heading straight toward his seat. A wave of nervous anticipation washed over him. Lo and behold, she took the seat right beside his. What luck!

Anxious to break the ice and strike up a conversation, he blurted out, "So, where are you flying today?"

She turned and smiled and said, "To the annual nymphomaniac convention in Chicago."

He swallowed hard, and was instantly crazed with excitement. Struggling to maintain his outward cool, he calmly asked, "And what's your role at this convention?"

She flipped her hair back, turned to him, locked onto his eyes, and said, "Well, I'm giving a lecture in which I'll try to debunk some of the popular myths about sexuality."

"Really," he said, swallowing hard. "And what myths are those?"

She explained, "Well, one popular myth is that African-American men are the most well endowed when, in fact, Native Americans are most likely to possess this trait. Another popular myth is that Frenchmen are the best lovers, when actually it is men of Jewish descent who romance women best, on average."

"Very interesting," the man responded.

Suddenly, the woman became embarrassed and blushed. "I'm sorry," she said, "I feel so awkward discussing this with you, and I don't even know your name."

The man extended his hand and replied, "Tonto. Tonto Goldstein."

Mendel the tailor was worried about his business. He was down to his last $50 and was torn between buying a sign and getting food for his family. Mendel decided to pray.

"Dear God," he said, "I don't know what to do. If I buy a sign it may bring in business, but I need to buy groceries for my family . . . and if the sign doesn't bring in sales, we will starve."

God replied, "Mendel, buy the sign. Don't worry, your family won't starve."

So Mendel bought the sign and business took off. The tailor fed his family and all was well. But as time passed, it became evident that Mendel couldn't keep up with the orders all by himself. He contemplated hiring an assistant, but wondered if he could afford it. So he asked God if getting help would be a prudent move.

"Go ahead," God tells Mendel, "hire some help, you'll do okay."

And so Mendel did as he was told by God. And business took off beyond his wildest dreams. After a time, the tailor decided to move to a larger site that would accommodate the growing demands of his business. As he surveyed certain locations, he found a perfect storefront, but the rental price was really steep.

"God," Mendel again implored, "I found the perfect place to relocate my business. But the cost of the lease worries me. I don't want to get in over my head."

"Go ahead and a get a lease on the store, Mendel," said God. "Trust me, you'll be okay—I haven't steered you wrong yet, have I?"

So Mendel signed a lease on the Fifth Avenue store and profits from his business went through the roof. Out of heartfelt gratitude for all the advice and care that God had rendered him, Mendel proposed to the Almighty that he dedicate the store to Him.

"How do you like the name 'Yaweh and Mendel,'" the tailor asked.

"Nah," God said. "Let's go with 'Lord and Taylor.'"

*　　*　　*

Mr. and Mrs. Shoenfeld were asleep in their beds late one night when Mrs. Shoenfeld heard a noise downstairs.

"Wake up!" cried Mrs. Shoenfeld, nudging her husband. "There are burglars in the kitchen. I think they're eating the pot roast I made tonight!"

"In that case," said Mr. Shoenfeld, "I sure hope they don't die in the house!"

A Jewish man went to eat at a Chinese restaurant and eventually found himself wondering whether there were any Chinese Jews. When the waiter came over to take his order, he asked, "Pardon me, but I'd like to know if there are any Chinese Jews?"

The waiter said, "I no know. I go into kitchen and ask manager."

After taking his order, the waiter went to the kitchen and returned in a few minutes. He earnestly explained to the man, "No. No Chinese Jews. We have orange Jews, tomato Jews, grape Jews, and pineapple Jews, but no Chinese Jews."

Meyer, a lonely widower, was walking home along Hester Street one day wishing something wonderful could happen in his life, when he passed a pet store and heard a squawking voice shouting out in Yiddish: "Quawwwwk . . . *vos macht du* . . . Yeah, *du* . . . outside, standing like a *putzel* . . . eh?"

Meyer rubbed his eyes and ears. He couldn't believe it. The proprietor sprang out of the door and grabbed Meyer by the sleeve. "Come in here, fella, and check out this parrot!"

Meyer stood in front of an African grey that cocked his little head and said: "*Vos? Kenst reddin Yiddish?*"

Meyer turned excitedly to the store owner. "He speaks Yiddish?"

"*Voh den?* Chinese maybe?"

In a matter of moments, Meyer had placed five hundred dollars down on the counter and carried the parrot in his cage away with him. All night he talked with the parrot—in Yiddish. He told the parrot about his father's adventures coming to America, about how beautiful his mother was when she was a young bride, about his family, about his years of working in the garment center.

The parrot listened and commented from time to time. They shared some walnuts. The parrot told him of living in the pet store, how he hated the weekends, and people who treated him like an idiot.

Next morning, Meyer began to put on his prayer shawl, all the while, saying his prayers. The parrot demanded to know what he was doing and when Meyer explained, the parrot wanted some, too. Meyer went out and handmade a miniature shawl for the parrot.

The parrot wanted to learn to daven, and he learned every prayer. He wanted to learn to read Hebrew so Meyer spent weeks and months, sitting and teaching the parrot, teaching him Torah. In time, Meyer came to love and count on the parrot as a friend and a Jew. He had been saved.

One morning, on Rosh Hashanah, Meyer rose and got dressed and was about to leave when the parrot demanded to go with him. Meyer explained that shul was not a place for a bird, but the parrot made a terrific argument and eventually was carried to shul on Meyer's shoulder.

Needless to say, they made quite a spectacle, and Meyer was questioned by everyone, including the rabbi and cantor. They refused to allow a bird into the building on the High Holy Days, but Meyer convinced them to let him in this one time, swearing the parrot could daven. Soon, congregationers began making wagers with Meyer. Thousands of dollars were bet (even odds) that the parrot could *not* daven, could not speak Yiddish or read Hebrew, etc.

All eyes were on the African grey during services. The parrot perched on Meyer's shoulder as one prayer and song passed. Meyer heard not a peep from the bird. He began to become annoyed, slapping at his shoulder and mumbling under his breath, "Daven!"

Nothing.

"Daven, parrot, you can daven, so daven. . . . Come on, everybody's looking at you!"

Nothing.

After Rosh Hashanah services were concluded, Meyer found that he owed his shul buddies and the rabbi over four thousand dollars. He marched home, furious, saying nothing.

Finally, several blocks from the temple, the bird began to sing an old Yiddish song and was happy as a lark. Meyer stopped and looked at him.

"You miserable bird! You cost me over four thousand dollars. Why? After I made your shawl and taught you the morning prayers, and taught you to read Hebrew and the Torah. And after you begged me to bring you to shul on Rosh Hashanah, why? Why did you do this to me?"

"Don't be an idiot," the parrot replied. "Think of the odds on Yom Kippur!"

Mr. Moskowitz had married off four of his children but the fifth was a problem. Young Jake had no visible virtues that would make him a desirable husband. He had neither good looks, charm, intelligence, manners, nor conversation. Yet it was unthinkable that he remain single. Moskowitz decided to call in a *shadchan*, a Jewish matchmaker.

The *shadchan* listened and said, "I have just the girl for the young man—Princess Anne."

"Who?"

"Princess Anne. The daughter of Queen Elizabeth the Second of Great Britain."

"A *shiksa*?!"

The *shadchan* sighed. "Why the prejudice? In these enlightened times, what's wrong with a Gentile girl? She comes from a good family, with very little anti-Semitism. They fought Hitler, if you'll remember. They have the very best social connections.

They're wealthy and the princess is a real beauty. See. I'll write the names down together."

Suiting action to words, he painstakingly wrote "Jacob Moskowitz" in his little book and right below it, "Princess Anne Mountbatten."

Moskowitz had to admit the names went well together, but he said, "You don't understand. I have to consider my old aunt. She is extremely pious. If she found out Jake was marrying a *shiksa* she'd go right out of her mind."

The *shadchan* put away his little book. "Let me talk to her."

An appointment was arranged, and for hours, quite literally hours, the matchmaker pleaded, stormed, raged, cajoled, and slowly broke down the old lady.

Her faded eyes awash with tears and her little chin trembling, the aunt said at last, "Well, maybe you're right and I shouldn't be so old-fashioned. If, as you say, she is a fine girl, and if she will make Jake happy, and if the children will be brought up Jewish, all right. For myself, I can always move out of town and change my name so no one will know my shame. Go ahead; I will make no objection."

The *shadchan* nodded gleefully and staggered out of the room. The session had worn him out and left him but a shell of his former self. Emerging into the street, he opened his little book to the page on which both names had been written. He put a firm checkmark after the name Jacob Moskowitz and said, with a huge and tremulous sigh of relief, "Half done!"

*   *   *

Seventy-two-year-old Matthew lay seriously ill. An old friend came to visit him.

"Wait, Matthew, you'll live to be eighty," he said, trying to comfort him. "God will see to that."

"What, do you think God can't add?" Matthew scoffed. "If he can get me at seventy-two, why should he wait until I'm eighty?"

A man was wandering around in a field, thinking about how good his wife had been to him, and how fortunate he was to have her.

He asked God, "Why did you make her so kindhearted?"

The Lord responded, "So you could love her, my son."

"Why did you make her so good-looking?"

"So you could love her, my son."

"Why did you make her such a good cook?"

"So you could love her, my son."

The man thought about this. Then he said, "I don't mean to seem ungrateful or anything, but why did you make her so stupid?"

"So she could love you, my son."

A totally hysterical woman ran all the way to the rabbi's house and tearfully appealed to his secretary, "Please, ask the rabbi to help find my husband—he ran away!"

The secretary wrote down her request and brought it to the

rabbi in his study. A moment later, he came out again and told the woman, "The rabbi wishes to assure you that your husband will return to you shortly."

"May God repay the rabbi a thousand times for his kindness!" cried the woman. And she went home.

After she had gone, the rabbi's secretary said to a few bystanders, "*Oy vay*, the poor woman! Her husband will never return to her."

"Don't you believe in what the rabbi says?" one of the bystanders asked in surprise.

"Of course I do!" answered the secretary. "But the rabbi saw only her petition. I saw her face!"

Two foolish men got involved in a rather philosophical argument.

"Since you're so wise," said one, sarcastically, "try to answer this question: Why is it that when a slice of buttered bread falls to the ground, it's bound to fall on the buttered side?"

But as the other sage was something of a scientist he decided to disprove this theory by a practical experiment. He went and buttered a slice of bread. Then he dropped it.

"There you are!" he cried triumphantly. "The bread, as you see, hasn't fallen on its buttered side at all. So where is your theory now?"

"Ho-ho!" laughed the other, derisively. "You think you're smart! You buttered the bread on the wrong side!"

*   *   *

The doctor was checking up on the health of his patient.

He consoled him as soon as he completed his examination. "Fine, fine, Mr. Schoenfeld, you're doing much better," he said. "Your general condition has improved. There is only one thing that doesn't look so good—your floating kidney. But that doesn't worry me a bit."

"And if you had a floating kidney," snapped Mr. Schoenfeld, "do you think *I'd* worry about it?"

David went to a kosher deli, where he ordered whitefish. After the waiter served him, he overheard David talking to the fish. Soon David was deep in conversation with his lunch.

The waiter came to the table. "So what's the deal here?" he asked. "You plan on eating it or taking it home and marrying it?"

"We're just schmoozing," says David. "Turns out the fish is from Great Neck Bay. I used to live there. So I was asking him how things are back in Great Neck."

"Oh, really! So what did the fish say?" asked the waiter.

"He said, 'How should I know? I ain't been there in years!'"

A thief was hanging around the stalls in an open food market. When the fish dealer was looking the other way, he picked up a big salmon and hid it under his coat.

As he was walking off, the fish dealer called after him: "Listen, uncle, the next time you steal a fish, be sure that either your coat is longer or the fish is shorter!"

Lying in his hospital bed, a dying man began to flail about and make motions as if he would like to speak.

The rabbi, keeping watch at the side of his bed, leaned quietly over and asked, "Do you have something you would like to say?"

The man nodded in the affirmative, and the rabbi handed him a pad and pen. "I know you can't speak, but use this to write a note and I will give it to your wife. She's waiting just outside."

Gathering his last bit of strength, the man took them and scrawled his message upon the pad, which he then stuffed into the rabbi's hands. Then, moments later, the man died.

After saying Kaddish, the rabbi left to break the sad news to the wife. After consoling her a bit, the rabbi handed her the note. "Here were his last words. Just before passing on, he wrote this message to you."

The wife tearfully opened the note, which read *"You're standing on my oxygen hose!!"*

A matchmaker cornered a yeshiva student and told him, "Do I have a girl for you!"

"Not interested," replied the student.

"But she's beautiful!" exclaimed the matchmaker.

"Yeah?" says the student.

"Yes. And she's very rich, too."

"Really?"

"And she has great ancestry! From a very fine family."

"Sounds great," the student admitted. "But why would a girl like that want to marry me? She'd have to be crazy."

The matchmaker said, "Well, you can't have everything!"

Mr. Cohen went to the doctor's office to collect his wife's test results.

The doctor's receptionist told him, "I'm sorry, sir, but there has been a bit of a mixup. We have a problem. When we sent your wife's samples to the lab, the samples from another Mrs. Cohen were sent as well, and we are now uncertain which one is your wife's. Frankly, that's either bad or terrible."

Mr. Cohen asked, "What do you mean?"

The receptionist sighed, "Well, one Mrs. Cohen has tested positive for Alzheimer's disease and the other for AIDS. We can't tell which is your wife."

"That's terrible! Can we do the test over?"

"Normally, yes. But your medical plan won't pay for these expensive tests more than once."

Mr. Cohen asked, "Well, what am I supposed to do now?"

The receptionist replied, "The doctor recommends that you drop your wife off somewhere in the middle of Brooklyn. If she finds her way home, don't sleep with her."

Sam Schwartz called his veterinarian, "Doctor, you've got to come right over! My dog just ate the TV remote control!"

"I'll be right there, Sam."

"Thanks, but what do I do in the meantime?"

The vet said, "Read a magazine."

An old homeless Jewish man stopped a well-dressed man on the street and implored him, "Please, mister, could you spare me maybe a quarter today?"

Angrily, the gentleman snapped, "I should say not! I don't go around handing out money to people on the street!"

"So what you want I should do," replied the old man, "open up an office?"

Two rabbinical students were caught by the rabbi gambling and drinking in the company of undesirable characters, even before the sun set on the evening of the Sabbath.

The rabbi called them into his study the next day. Both confessed to having given in to weakness, and admitted that they deserved punishment. The rabbi thought and then went into his kitchen and brought back two bags of dried peas. "Put these in your shoes," he told them, "and walk on them for a week, to remind yourself how hard life can be when you turn away from the Law."

A few days later the two students met. One was limping terribly, had dark circles under his eyes, and looked very tired. The other seemed much as he had been the week before.

"Hey," said the first. "How is it that you're walking so freely. Didn't you do as the rabbi told us and put the peas in your shoes?"

"Of course I did," said the other. "How could I disobey the rabbi?" He started to walk away, then paused and said, "But I boiled them first."

"Doctor, I need your help," complained Yoitle. "I talk to myself!"

"Do you suffer any pain?" asked the doctor.

"No."

"In that case," said the doctor, "go home and don't worry. Millions of people talk to themselves."

"But Doctor," cried Yoitle, "you don't know what a nudnik I am!"

A matchmaker went to see Mr. Cohen, a confirmed bachelor for many years.

"Mr. Cohen, don't leave it too late. I have exactly the one you need. You only have to say the word and you'll meet and be married in no time!" said the matchmaker.

"Don't bother," replied Mr. Cohen, "I've two sisters at home, who look after all my needs."

"That's all well and good, but all the sisters in the world cannot fill the role of a wife."

"I said 'two sisters.' I didn't say they were mine!"

Goldie and Harold were driving in San Francisco in their aged Oldsmobile and Goldie was at the wheel. They were at the top of California Street, in the hilly and fancy financial district, when all of a sudden the brakes failed. Goldie pressed the brake pedal so hard it nearly went through the floor. Then she nearly tore the hand brake out by the roots as she wove in and out of the cars going down the hill at an ever-increasing speed.

"*Oy vay!*" Goldie wailed. "Harry, what should I do!!"

"For God's sake!" Harry screamed. "Hit something cheap!"

An old Jew and a young Jew are traveling on the train. The young Jew asks: "Excuse me, what time is it?"

The old Jew does not answer.

"Excuse me, sir, what time is it?"

Still the old Jew keeps silent.

"Sir, I'm asking you what time it is. Why don't you answer?!"

The old Jew says: "Son, the next stop is the last on this route. I don't know you, so you must be a stranger. If I answer you now, I'll have to invite you to my home. You're handsome, and I have a beautiful daughter. You will both fall in love and you will want to get married. Tell me, why would I need a son-in-law who can't even afford a watch?"

It was just two days before Passover, and the rich Jewish banker was furious with his tailor for taking so long to finish his new suit.

"Well," he ranted, "it certainly took you long enough! I was beginning to wonder if I would have to go to the synagogue in my old clothes. Now spread out the suit and let me see what kind of a job you did. I demand absolute perfection, as you know!"

The tailor meekly displayed the new three-piece suit.

After he had carefully inspected the coat, the vest, and the trousers, the banker finally softened, for the new suit was, indeed, beautifully made. "If only you hadn't taken so long," he said in a milder tone. "You know, it only took the Lord six days to make this entire world of ours, while it took you two entire weeks to make this three-piece suit."

"That's true," replied the tailor, "but look at my suit of clothes, and look at this world. Don't you think the good Lord could have taken another week?"

One day a man walks into a dentist's office and asks how much it will cost to extract wisdom teeth.

"Eighty dollars," the dentist says.

"That's a ridiculous amount," the man says. "Isn't there a cheaper way?"

"Well," the dentist says, "if you don't use an anesthetic, I can knock it down to sixty dollars. But it will be pretty painful."

"That's still too expensive," the man says. "It doesn't matter how painful it is."

"Okay," says the dentist. "If I save on anesthesia and simply rip the teeth out with a pair of pliers, I could get away with charging twenty dollars. But that could be more pain than you can stand."

"Nope," moans the man, "it's still too much money."

"Hmm," says the dentist, scratching his head. "If I let one of my students do it for the experience, I suppose I could charge you just ten dollars."

"Marvelous," says the man, "book my wife for next Tuesday!"

Two Jewish men, Mr. Cohen and Mr. Abraham, sat down in a smart kosher restaurant and a snooty waiter came over to take their order.

"Sirs, what can I get you?" inquired the waiter.

"A glass of orange juice," said Mr. Cohen.

"A glass of orange juice for me, too," said Mr. Abraham, "but please make sure the glass is clean."

The waiter stalked off in a disagreeable manner, and eventually returned with two glasses of orange juice.

"So," he asked, "which one of you wanted the clean glass?"

Ten Things Jewish Men Know About Women

1.
2.
3.
4.
5.
6.
7.
8.
9.
10.

What does a Jewish husband call a water bed?
The Dead Sea.

*　　*　　*

A young Jewish student prided himself on his ability to confuse the wisest of scholars. Once, when he was surrounded by his friends, he sought to prove his self-asserted cleverness. He asked the town sage, "What was the first thing Eve did when Adam came home late one night?"

The sage responded, "She counted his ribs."

A Jewish father, Moishe, got a call from his eldest son, Yitzak, who told him, "Father, I am going to marry!"

Moishe actually danced with joy. "Tell me, is she a good Jewish girl? What's her name?"

"O'Brien," replied the son. "She's Catholic."

"*Oy!*" said the father. "But are you happy, my son?"

"I'm happy," said the son.

"Okay, as long as you're happy. My blessings to you both."

Now the father was counting more than ever on his remaining sons, Schlemiel and Chutzpah, to give him Jewish grandsons.

The next evening, Schlemiel called his father. "I, too, will soon be married, Father."

Again Moishe broke out into a dance and sang God's praises. "Pray, what is her name?" he asked.

"Kazalopodopolous," replied the son. "She's Greek Orthodox."

"*Oy!*" cried Moishe. "But are you happy?"

"I'm very happy, Father."

"Okay. Then you, too, have my blessing," Moishe declared.

Dejected, Moishe went to the temple to pray. "Please, God, let my remaining son, Chutzpah, marry a nice Jewish girl, to raise nice Jewish children in Your eyes . . . *please!*"

The next day, Chutzpah came to his father in quite a state. "Father! I am to wed in the spring!"

"Her *name? What is her name?*" his father immediately demanded.

"Goldberg!" replied Chutzpah.

Moishe was beside himself with joy. He leapt into the air and shouted, "Praise God! Praise the Prophets!"

When he calmed down sufficiently, he asked Chutzpah, "Is she Dr. Goldberg's daughter Shelley, from Newark?"

"No," replied Chutzpah.

"Hmm. Must be Attorney General Goldberg's daughter Rachel, from Hollywood."

"Ah, no, Father," Chutzpah again responded.

"Well then, what is her first name, my youngest, truest, most beautiful son?"

"Whoopi," Chutzpah replied.

Moshe went to see his supervisor in the front office.

"Boss," he said, "we're doing some heavy-duty house cleaning at home tomorrow for Pesach, and my wife needs me to help with the attic and the garage, moving and hauling stuff."

"We're shorthanded, Moshe," the boss replies. "I can't give you the day off."

"Thanks, boss," says Moshe, "I knew I could count on you!"

*   *   *

The crowded cafeteria sported a large sign reading: "Watch Your Hat and Overcoat."

Meyer did. He kept turning around every minute, almost choking over his food. His pal, Moshe, kept on eating, without thought of his own coat on the hook behind him. Finally Moshe said, "You, dope! Stop watching our overcoats."

"I'm only watching mine," replied Meyer. "Yours has been gone for over half an hour."

Sadie's husband, Jake, had been slipping in and out of a coma for several months, yet his faithful wife stayed by his bedside day and night.

One night, Jake comes to and motions for her to come closer. He said, "My Sadie, you have been with me through all the bad times. When I got fired, you were there to support me. When my business failed, you were there. When I got shot, you were by my side. When we lost the house, you gave me support. When my health started failing, you were still by my side. You know what, Sadie?"

"What dear?" she asked gently.

"I think you're bad luck."

It was a sweltering August day when the three Cohen brothers entered the posh Dearborn, Michigan, offices of Henry Ford, the esteemed car maker. "Mr. Ford," announced Norman Cohen, the eldest of the three, "we have a remarkable invention that will revolutionize the automobile industry."

Ford looked skeptical, but their threat to offer it to the competition kept his interest piqued.

"We would like to demonstrate it to you in person," Norman continued.

After a little cajoling, they brought Mr. Ford outside and asked him to enter a black automobile parked in front of the building. Hyman Cohen, the middle brother, opened the door of the car.

"Please step inside, Mr. Ford."

"What?!" shouted the tycoon. "Are you crazy? It must be two hundred degrees in that car!"

"It is," smiled the youngest brother, Max, "but sit down, Mr. Ford, and push the white button."

Intrigued, Ford pushed the button. All of a sudden a whoosh of freezing air started blowing from vents all around the car, and within seconds the automobile was not only comfortable, it was quite cool.

"This is amazing!" exclaimed Ford. "How much do you want for the patent?"

Norman spoke up, "The price is one million dollars." Then he paused. "And there is something else. The name 'Cohen Brothers Air-Conditioning' must be stamped right next to the Ford logo!"

"Money is no problem," retorted Ford, "but there is no way I will have a Jewish name next to my logo on my cars!"

They haggled back and forth for a while and finally they settled. Five million dollars, but the Cohens' name would be left

off. However, the first names of the Cohen brothers would be forever emblazoned upon the console of every Ford air-conditioning
system.

And that is why even today, whenever you enter a Ford
vehicle, you will see those three names clearly printed on the air-
conditioning control panel: NORM, HI, and MAX.

A cantor bragged before his congregation in a booming, bel-
lowing voice: "Two years ago I insured my voice with Lloyds of
London for $750,000."

There was a hushed and awed silence in the crowded room.

Suddenly, from the back of the room, a snappy elderly woman
asked, "So what did you do with the money?"

Yankel was pushing twenty-five and he'd never even been out
on a date. His rabbi called him into the office one day and said,
"Yankel! What's it going to be already? What are you waiting
for?"

Yankel blushed and explained to his rabbi that he'd grown up
in a house full of brothers, and he had never even spoken to a girl
anywhere near his age. He felt he wouldn't know what to say to
girls. Besides, to date would interrupt his learning.

The rabbi put a fatherly arm around him and told him, "Don't
worry about your learning. Learning always progresses. And as
for what to talk about with a young woman, well, you can talk
about her family, you can talk about what she likes, and if all else
fails you can talk philosophy."

Yankel left the rabbi, repeating under his breath, "Family, likes, philosophy. Family, likes, philosophy. Family, likes, philosophy."

Finally, the day arrived and he went out on his first date with a young woman from his congregation, arranged by the rabbi.

Yankel and his date sat in the hotel lobby and looked at each other uncomfortably. Yankel realized that he would have to say something, so he went to the first item on the rabbi's list, blurting out: "Do you have any brothers?"

"No," replied the young lady, and silence reigned again.

Yankel thought hard, and then came up with, "Do you like baseball?"

"No," came the immediate reply.

Now Yankel was really at a loss. Ah yes! Philosophy! Yankel leaned forward, and very intently, in his best talmudic tones, asked, "If you had a brother, would he like baseball?"

Three men were discussing their previous night's lovemaking.

The Italian said, "My wife, I rubbed her all over with fine olive oil, then we make wonderful love. She screamed for five minutes."

The Frenchman said, "I smooth sweet butter on my wife's body, then we made passionate love. She screamed for half an hour."

The Jew said, "I covered my wife's body with schmaltz. We made love and she screamed for six hours."

The others cried, "Six hours? How did you make her scream for six hours?"

He shrugged. "I wiped my hands on the drapes."

Goldblatt was showing off, as usual. He told his friend, "I bought a hearing aid yesterday. It cost me two thousand bucks, but it is state of the art. Digital, invisible, and I can hear *everything*."

"What kind is it?" his friend asked.

"A quarter of twelve," Goldblatt replied.

Irwin Sternmeyer was just coming out of anesthesia after a series of tests in the hospital, and his wife, Zelda, was sitting at his bedside. His eyes fluttered open, and he murmured, "You're beautiful."

Flattered, Zelda continued her vigil while he drifted back to sleep. Later he woke up and said, "You're cute."

"What happened to 'beautiful'?" Zelda asked.

"The drugs are wearing off," he replied.

A Jewish gentleman, fresh out of gift ideas, bought his mother-in-law a large plot in a very expensive cemetery. On her next birthday, he bought her nothing. She was quick to comment loud and long on his thoughtlessness.

"Well," he responded, "you haven't used the gift I gave you last year."

*   *   *

Adam was wandering around the Garden of Eden feeling very lonely.

God asked him, "What's wrong, Adam?"

Adam said he didn't have anyone to talk to.

God thought for a minute and then said that He was going to make him a companion and that it would be called "wonderful." "Wonderful will gather food for you, cook for you, agree with your every decision, bear your children, never ask you to get up in the middle of the night to take care of them, never nag you, be the first to admit being wrong when you've had a disagreement, and wonderful will never give you a headache."

Adam inquired, "What will wonderful cost?"

God replied, "An arm and a leg."

Adam asked, "What can I get for a rib?"

For his birthday, David received a parrot as a gift. This parrot was fully grown with a bad attitude and worse vocabulary. Every other word was an expletive. Those that weren't expletives were, to say the least, rude.

David tried hard to change the bird's attitude and was constantly saying polite words, playing soft music, anything that came to mind. Nothing worked. He yelled at the bird, the bird got worse. He shook the bird and the bird got even madder and ruder.

Finally, in a moment of desperation, David put the parrot in the freezer. For a few moments he heard the bird squawking, kicking, and screaming and then, suddenly, all was quiet.

David was frightened that he might have actually hurt the bird and quickly opened the freezer door.

The parrot calmly stepped out onto David's extended arm and said: "I'm sorry that I offended you with my language and actions. I ask for your forgiveness. I will try to change my behavior. . . ."

David was astounded at the bird's change in attitude and was about to ask what changed him when the parrot continued, "May I ask what the chicken did?"

A father went to visit his future son-in-law, who he finds deeply involved in studying Torah. He sits down and asks the boy, "So, son, what are you going to do to make a living?"

"I will study Torah and God will provide," the young man replied.

"I see. Well, how are you going to provide for my daughter?"

"I will study Torah and God will provide," he answered.

"And what about kids? Who's going to support them?!"

"I will study Torah and God will provide."

When the father arrived home later that afternoon, his wife met him at the door.

"So what did you find out about our new son-in-law?" she asked.

The father answered, "He has no job and no plans. But the good news is, he thinks I'm God."

Howard and Alex are strolling home from shul one Saturday morning. Suddenly a cab speeds past, and their friend, Irving, is running frantically behind it, flailing his arms wildly.

"Well," said Alex, "I never imagined our good friend Irving was a Sabbath violator! Look at him running for that taxi."

"Wait a minute," Howard replied. "Didn't you read that book I lent you, *The Other Side of the Story*, about the command to judge other people favorably? I'll bet we can think of hundreds of reasons for Irving's behavior."

"Yeah, like what?"

"Maybe he's sick and needs to go to the hospital."

"Come on! He was running sixty miles an hour after that cab—he's healthier than Arnold Schwartzenweiss," Alex declared.

"Well, maybe his wife's having a baby."

"She had one last week."

"Well, maybe he needs to visit her in the hospital," Howard offered.

"She's home."

"Well, maybe he's running to the hospital to get a doctor."

"He *is* a doctor."

"Well, maybe he need supplies from the hospital."

"The hospital is a three-minute walk in the opposite direction."

"Well, maybe he forgot that it's *Shabbos*!" Howard cried.

"Of course he knows it's *Shabbos*. Didn't you see his tie. It was his paisley beige one hundred percent silk Giovanni tie from Italy. He never wears it during the week."

"Wow, you're a really observant Jew! I didn't even notice he was wearing a tie."

"How could you not notice?" Alex asked. "Didn't you see how it was caught on the back fender of the taxi?"

The Hebrew school teacher was explaining how Lot's wife looked back and turned into a pillar of salt, when little David interrupted.

"My Mommy looked back once while she was *driving*," he announced triumphantly, "and she turned into a telephone pole!"

A guy got a new dog and he couldn't wait to show him off to his neighbor. When the neighbor finally came over, the guy called the dog into the house, bragging about how smart the creature was. The dog quickly came running and stood looking up at his master, tail wagging furiously, mouth open in a classic doggie smile, eyes bright with anticipation.

The guy pointed to the newspaper rolled up on the couch and commanded, "Fetch!"

Immediately, the dog sat down, the tail-wagging stopped, and the doggie smile disappeared. He hung his head, looked balefully up at his master, and said in a whiny voice, "*Oy!* My tail hurts from wagging so much and that dog food you're feeding me tastes absolutely terrible. And I can't remember the last time you took me out for a walk. . . . "

The neighbor looks puzzled.

"Oh," explained the dog owner, "he thought I said 'Kvetch!' "

Mr. Cohen was brought to the emergency room at Mercy Hospital and taken quickly in for coronary surgery. The operation went well and as the groggy man regained consciousness, he was reassured by the doctor who was waiting by his bed.

"You're going to be just fine, Mr. Cohen," the doctor said.

The doctor was joined by a nurse who said, "We do need to know, however, how you intend to pay for your stay here. Are you covered by insurance?"

Mr. Cohen said, "No, I'm not," in a whisper.

"Then can you pay in cash?" the nurse persisted.

"I'm afraid I cannot."

"Well, do you have any close relatives?" the nurse questioned sternly.

"Just my sister in New York," he volunteered. "But she converted to . . . she's a nun . . . in fact a real spinster."

"Oh, I must correct you, Mr. Cohen. Nuns are not spinsters—they are married to God."

"Wonderful, wonderful," Mr. Cohen said. "In that case, please send my bill to my brother-in-law."

*   *   *

An elderly man went to the doctor complaining of aches and pains all over his body. After a thorough examination, the doctor gives him a clean bill of health.

"Hymie, you're in fine shape for an eighty-year-old. After all, I'm not a magician—I can't make you any younger," said the doctor.

"Who asked you to make me younger? Just make sure I get older!"

JEWISH MOTHERS

In his seminal humorous 1965 bestseller How to Be a Jewish Mother, *Dan Greenburg correctly wrote that you didn't have to be Jewish, or even female, to be a Jewish mother: An Italian barber can be a Jewish mother. Beyond this important remark, in American culture, Jewish mothers are so ubiquitous in and out of humorous contexts that they scarcely need an introduction.*

*　　*　　*

Of course, Jewish mothers merit a chapter of their own. . . .

What's the difference between a rottweiler and a Jewish mother?
Eventually, the rottweiler lets go.

A man calls his mother in Florida. "Mom, how are you?"
"Not too good," says the mother. "I've been very weak."
The son says, "Why are you so weak?"
She says, "Because I haven't eaten in thirty-eight days."

The man says, "That's terrible. Why haven't you eaten in thirty-eight days?"

The mother answers, "Because I didn't want my mouth to be filled with food if you should call."

Why don't Jewish mothers drink?
Alcohol interferes with their suffering.

A young Jewish man was seeing a psychiatrist for an eating and sleeping disorder. "I am so obsessed with my mother. . . . As soon as I go to sleep, I start dreaming, and everyone in my dream turns into my mother. I wake up in such a state, all I can do is go downstairs and eat a piece of toast."

The psychiatrist replies: "What, just one piece of toast, for a big boy like you?"

One day a Jewish mother and her eight-year-old daughter were walking along the beach, just at the water's edge. Suddenly, a gigantic wave flashed up on the beach and swept the little girl out to sea.

"Oh, God," lamented the mother, turning her face toward heaven and shaking her fist. "This was my *only* baby. I can't have more children. She is the love and joy of my life. I have cherished every day that she's been with me. Give her back to me, and I'll go to the synagogue every day for the rest of my life!"

Suddenly, another huge wave flashed up and deposited the girl back on the sand next to her mother.

The mother looked up to heaven and said, "She was wearing a *hat!*"

Three Jewish mothers were sitting on a park bench.

The first one let out a heartfelt *"Oy!"*

A few minutes later, the second sighed deeply and said, *"Oy vay!"*

A few minutes after that, the third lady brushed away a tear and moans, *"Oy vay iz mir!"*

To which the first lady said, "I thought we agreed we weren't going to talk about our children!"

Young Marvin went to Boy Scout camp. During inspection, the scoutmaster found an umbrella in his bedroll.

"What's this doing here?" he yelled. "This isn't listed as a necessary item."

"Maybe not," Marvin replied, "but you obviously don't have a Jewish mother."

Why aren't Jewish mothers ever attacked by sharks?
Professional courtesy.

Did you hear about the bum who walked up to the Jewish mother on the street and said, "Lady, I haven't eaten in three days."

"Force yourself," she replied.

What's a genius?
An average student with a Jewish mother.

Mama's Hanukkah Letter

Dear Darling Son and That Person You Married,

Happy Hanukkah to you, and please don't worry. I'm just fine considering I can't breathe or eat. The important thing is that you have a nice holiday, thousands of miles away from your ailing mother. I've sent along my last ten dollars in this card, which I hope you'll spend on my grandchildren.

God knows their mother never buys them anything nice. They look so thin in their pictures, poor babies.

Well, son, it's time for me to crawl off to bed now. I lost my cane fending off muggers last week, but don't you worry about me. I'm also getting used to the cold since they turned my heat off and am grateful because the frost on my bed numbs the constant pain. Now don't you even think about sending any more money, because I know you need it for those expensive family vacations you take every year. Give my love to my darling grandbabies and my regards to whatever-her-name-is—the one with the black roots who stole you screaming from my bosom.

Happy Hanukkah,
Love, Mom

What did the Jewish mother ask her daughter when the daughter told her she had had an affair?

Who catered it?

*   *   *

Three sons of a *Yiddishe* momma left their homeland, went abroad, and prospered. They discussed the gifts they were able to give their old mother for her seventy-fifth birthday.

Avraham, the first, said: "I built a big house for our mother."

Moishe, the second, said: "I sent her a Mercedes with a driver."

David, the youngest, said: "You remember how our mother enjoys reading the Bible. Now she can't see very well. I sent her a remarkable parrot that recites the whole Bible—Momma just has to name the chapter and verse."

Soon thereafter, a letter of thanks came to the three sons from their mother.

"Avraham," she said, "the house you built is so huge. I live only in one room, but I have to clean the whole house.

"Moishe," she continued, "I am too old to travel. I stay most of the time at home, so I rarely use the Mercedes. And that driver has *shpilkes*—he's a pain in the *toches*."

"But David," she said, "the chicken was *delicious*!"

Why do Jewish mothers make such terrible parole officers?
They never let anyone finish a sentence.

Two Jewish mothers were sitting under hair dryers at the hairdresser.

The first asks the other, "So *nu*, how's your family?"

The second responds, "Oh, just fine. My daughter is married to the most wonderful man. She never has to cook, he always takes her out. She never has to clean, he got her a housekeeper. She never has to work, he's got such a good job. She never has to worry about the children, he got her a nanny."

She continues with a question to the first lady, "So, how is your son these days?"

The first woman says, "Just awful. He is married to such a witch of a woman. She makes him take her out to dinner every night, she never cooks a dish. She made him get her a house-keeper, God forbid she should vacuum a carpet! He has to work like a dog because she won't get a job and she never takes care of their children, because she made him get her a nanny!"

Rachel and Esther meet for the first time in fifty years since high school.

Rachel began to tell Esther about her children. "My son is a doctor and he's got four kids. My daughter is married to a lawyer and they have three great kids. So tell me, Esther, how about your kids?"

Esther replies, "Unfortunately, Morty and I don't have any children and so we have no grandchildren either."

Rachel says, "No children? And no grandkids? So tell me, Esther, what do you do for aggravation?"

What is the difference between an Italian mother whose son won't eat her cooking and a Jewish mother whose son won't eat her cooking?

The Italian mother kills her son; the Jewish mother kills herself.

The time came for a Jewish mother to send her son off to his first day of school. She showered him with customary pride and precautionary advice: "So, *bubeleh,* you'll be a good boy and listen to the teacher? And you won't make noise, *bubeleh,* and you'll be very polite and play nice with the other children. And when it's time to come home, you'll button up warm, so you won't catch cold, *bubeleh.* And you'll be careful crossing the street and come straight home. . . . " And on and on.

Off to school the little boy went.

When he returned that afternoon, his mother hugged him and kissed him and exclaimed, "So, did you like school, *bubeleh?* You made new friends? You learned something?"

"Yeah," replied the boy. "I learned my name is Irving."

Twenty-Five Comebacks to the Age-Old Jewish Mother Question: "Why aren't you married yet?"

1. You haven't asked yet.
2. I was hoping to do something meaningful with my life.
3. What? And spoil my great sex life?
4. Nobody would believe me in white.
5. Because I just love hearing this question.
6. Just lucky, I guess.
7. It gives my mother something to live for.

8. My fiancé(e) is awaiting his (her) parole.

9. I'm still hoping for a shot at Miss/Mr. America.

10. Do you know how hard it is to get two tickets to *The Producers*?

11. I'm waiting until I get to be your age.

12. It didn't seem worth a blood test.

13. I already have enough laundry to do, thank you.

14. Because I think it would take all the spontaneity out of dating.

15. My co-op board doesn't allow spouses.

16. I'd have to forfeit my billion-dollar trust fund.

17. They just opened a great singles bar on my block.

18. I wouldn't want my parents to drop dead from sheer happiness.

19. I guess it just goes to prove that you can't trust those voodoo doll rituals.

20. What? And lose all the money I've invested in running personal ads?

21. We really want to, but my lover's spouse just won't go for it.

22. I don't want to have to support another person on my paycheck.

23. Why aren't you thin?

24. I'm married to my career, although recently we have been considering a trial separation.

25. (Bonus reply for single mothers) Because having a husband and a child would be redundant.

A young Jewish man excitedly told his mother that he'd fallen in love and was going to get married. He said, "And just for fun, Ma, I'm going to bring over three women and you try and guess which one I'm going to marry."

The mother agreed.

The next day, he brought three beautiful women into the house and sat them down on the couch. They chatted with each other and his mother for a while.

Finally, the man said, "Okay, Ma. Guess which one I'm going to marry."

She immediately replied, "The redhead in the middle."

"That's amazing, Ma! You're right. How did you know?"

"I don't like her."

What did the waiter ask the table of ten Jewish mothers?
"Is *anything* all right?"

A young gay man suddenly called home and told his Jewish mother that he had met a wonderful girl and that they were going to be married. He told his mother that he assumed she would be happier now, because he knew she'd been very disturbed about his homosexuality.

She responded that she was indeed delighted and asked tentatively, "I suppose it would be too much to hope that she would be Jewish?"

He told her that not only is the girl Jewish, but from a wealthy Beverly Hills family. The mother admitted she was overwhelmed by the news, and asked, "What is her name?"

He answered, "Monica Lewinsky."

There was a pause, then his mother asked, "What happened to that nice black boy you were dating last year?"

*   *   *

A young Jewish man calls his mother and says, "Mom, I'm bringing home a wonderful woman I want to marry. She's a Native American and her name is Shooting Star."

"How nice," says his mother.

"I have an Indian name, too," he says. "It's Running Deer and I want you to call me that from now on."

"How nice," says his mother.

"You should have an Indian name, too, Mom," he says.

"I already do," says the mother. "You should call me Sitting Shiva."

Two Jewish women were discussing their sons, each of whom was incarcerated in the state prison.

The first woman said, "*Oy*, my son has it so hard. He is locked away in maximum security, he never even speaks to anyone or sees the light of day. He has no exercise and he lives a horrible life."

The second said, "Well, my son is in minimum security. He exercises every day, he spends time in the prison library, takes some classes, and writes home each week."

"*Oy*," says the first woman, "you must get such *naches* from your son."

Things a Jewish Mother Would Never Say

"Just live with him . . . you don't have to marry him. I don't need any grandchildren."

"Be good and for your birthday I'll buy you a motorcycle!"

"How on earth can you see the TV, sitting so far back?"

"Don't bother wearing a jacket—it's quite warm out."

"Let me smell that shirt—yeah, it's good for another week."

"I think a cluttered bedroom is a sign of creativity."

"Yeah, I used to skip school, too."

"Just leave all the lights on . . . it makes the house more cheery."

"Could you turn the music up louder, so I can enjoy it, too?"

"Run and bring me the scissors! Hurry!"

"Aw, just turn these undies inside out. No one will ever know."

"I don't have a tissue with me—just use your sleeve."

"Well, if Timmy's mom says it's okay, that's good enough for me."

"Of course you should walk to school and back. What's the big deal about having to cross a few main streets?"

"My meeting won't be over till later tonight. You kids don't mind skipping dinner, do you?"

"I saw your subscription to Playboy *was expiring so I sent in a check to renew."*

"If she wants you both to move back east to live near her family it's fine with me."

"Mother's Day, Shmother's Day, you just go to the beach and enjoy yourselves."

"You don't have to call me every week! I know how busy you are."

"Your father is a saint; you should only be just like him."

"You are so lucky to have your in-laws."

"Your wife knows best—forget any advice I ever gave you and ask her what to do."

*   *   *

Harry Goldberg has been elected the next president of the United States—the first Jewish boy to reach the White House. He is very proud and phones his mother in New York to invite her to the inauguration.

"Momma, guess what!" he cried. "I've just been elected president. You've got to come to my inauguration."

"Harry! You know I hate trains. I can't face the journey all the way to Washington. Maybe next time."

"Momma! You will take no train. Air Force One will collect you. The journey will be over in thirty minutes. Come to my inauguration, please, for the love of God!"

"Harry, I hate hotels. The nonkosher food! Nahh, maybe next time."

"Momma! You will stay in the White House, a kosher chef to yourself. *Please* come."

"Harry! I have nothing to wear!"

"I have someone on his way to take you to Macy's and Bloomingdale's to make you look perfect. You must come!"

"Okay, okay, I suppose I will come."

Inauguration Day soon arrives. Mother is in the front row, next to the secretary of state. Harry is called up to become the next president. Mother digs the secretary of state in the ribs and says, "Hey, you see that boy Harry? His brother is a very successful doctor!"

If They'd Had a Jewish Mother . . .

Mona Lisa's mother: "After all that money your father and I spent on braces, that's the biggest smile you can give us?"

Christopher Columbus's mother: "I don't care what you've discovered, you still could have written!"

Michelangelo's mother: "Can't you paint on walls like other children? Do you have any idea how hard it is to get that stuff off the ceiling?"

Abraham Lincoln's mother: "Again with the stovepipe hat? Can't you just wear a baseball cap like the other kids?"

Albert Einstein's mother: "But it's your senior picture. Can't you do something about your hair? Styling gel, mousse, something . . . ?"

George Washington's mother: "The next time I catch you throwing money across the Potomac, you can kiss your allowance good-bye!"

Jonah's mother: "That's a nice story. Now tell me where you've really been for the last forty years."

Paul Revere's mother: "I don't care where you think you have to go, young man, midnight is past your curfew."

Three Jewish mothers were sitting around and bragging about their children. The first one said, "You know my son, he graduated first in his class from Stanford, he's now a doctor making $250,000 a year in Chicago."

The second woman said, "You know my son, he graduated first

in his class from Harvard, he's now a lawyer making half a million dollars a year and he lives in Los Angeles."

The last woman said, "You know my son, he never did too well in school, he never went to any university but he now makes a million dollars a year in New York working as a sports repairman."

The other two women asked: "What's a sports repairman?"

The third woman replied, "He fixes hockey games, football games, baseball games. . . . "

One day, Glenn invited his mother over for dinner. During the course of the meal, Glenn's mother couldn't help but notice how beautiful Glenn's roommate, Debbie, was.

Mrs. Sauerstein had long suspected that Glenn was involved in a romantic relationship with Debbie, and now she was even more suspicious.

Over the course of the evening, while watching the two interact, Mrs. Sauerstein started to wonder if there was more between Glenn and his roommate than met the eye. Reading his mom's thoughts, Glenn volunteered, "I know what you must be thinking, but I assure you Debbie and I are just roommates."

About a week later, Debbie came to Glenn saying, "Ever since your mother came to dinner, I've been unable to find the beautiful silver gravy ladle. You don't suppose she took it, do you?"

Glenn said, "Well, I doubt it, but I'll write her a letter just to be sure." So he sat down and wrote:

Dear Mother,

I'm not saying that you "did" take the gravy ladle from the house, I'm not saying that you "did not" take the gravy ladle. But the fact remains that one has been missing ever since you were here for dinner.

Several days later, Glenn received a letter from his mother, which read:

Dear Son,

I'm not saying that you "do" sleep with Debbie, and I'm not saying that you "do not" sleep with Debbie. But the fact remains that if she were sleeping in her own bed, she would have found the gravy ladle by now.

Love,
Mom

Rita was having a horrible day. Her nerves were shot. When the phone rang, she lunged for it, and listened with some relief to the kindly voice.

"Darling, how are you? This is Momma."

"Oh, Momma," she said, "I'm having a bad day." Breaking into bitter tears, she continued, "The baby won't eat and the washing machine broke down. I haven't had a chance to go shopping, and besides, I've just sprained my ankle and I have to hobble around. On top of that, the house is a mess and I'm supposed to have the Kirshners and Ginsbergs for dinner tonight."

"Darling, let Momma handle it. Sit down, relax, and close your eyes. I'll be over in half an hour. I'll do your shopping, clean up the house, and cook your dinner for you. I'll feed the baby and I'll call a repairman I know who'll be at your house to fix the washing machine promptly. Now stop crying. I'll do everything. In fact, I'll even call Morty at the office and tell him he ought to come home and help his wife out for once."

"Morty?" said Rita. "Who's Morty?"

"Why, Morty's your husband! . . . Is this 223-1374?"

"No, this is 223-1375."

"Oh, I'm sorry. I guess I have the wrong number."

There was a short pause, then Rita said, "Does this mean you're not coming over?"

Three Jewish mothers were talking rather competitively about how much their sons love them.

The first one said, "My son loves me so much, he spent a hundred dollars on flowers he sent me the other day."

The second one declared, "My son loves me so much, he paid for my trip to Europe last month."

The third one said, "My son loves me most. He goes to a therapist twice a week, paying five hundred dollars a visit, and all he talks about is me!"

JEWISH
GRANDMOTHERS

Jewish grandmothers are more than merely Jewish mothers to the tenth power, they are a force of nature, to be respected, feared, and reckoned with. Naturally, they are also a force to be lampooned.

*   *   *

A Jewish Grandmother's Guide to the Proper Preparation of Gefilte Fish

Two weeks before any major Jewish holiday, phone your daughter and ask her what she's planning to serve at the festive meal. Express your revulsion and outrage when she suggests serving bottled gefilte fish. Offer to make the fish yourself, but urge your daughter to take a day off from work so that she can watch you make the fish, so she'll know how to make it for her kids after she has put you in The Home.

One day before the holiday, call your daughter and tell her

that you hate to disappoint her, but you simply don't have the strength to make gefilte fish.

While your daughter is racing all over looking for some sort of a substitute appetizer, get all dressed up and take a bus, then a subway, then another bus, all the way to an obscure fish store in a slum where they still sell *live carp.*

Examine the carp swimming in the fish tank. Ask the owner if any fresher carp will be arriving soon. Ask him how often he changes the water.

On principle, reject the first two fish that he offers you. Accept fish only after the third or fourth.

Lugging two heavy shopping bags filled with fish and ice packs, take three buses home, unless someone has told you about a way of taking four.

Call your daughter as soon as you get home and tell her that you felt a little bit better and decided to go to your special fish store to pick up the carp. You know how busy she is right before the holidays so you didn't want to ask her to drive all the way out there.

Sigh and tell her how exhausted you are. Describe in vivid detail the assassin who tried to steal your pocketbook as you were boarding the third bus. Inquire whether your daughter would mind picking you up. You normally wouldn't ask but it's much easier to make the gefilte fish in her kitchen because she has all the latest electric gadgets.

As soon as you get to her kitchen, remove several washed mixing bowls from your daughter's dishwasher and, while she's watching, then rinse them to make sure they're clean.

There should be a separate bowl for each ingredient so that dirt from the carrots will not get on the celery. Put the diced carrots in one bowl, the sliced celery in the second, the chopped onions in the third, and then combine them all in a fourth bowl. Keep telling your daughter to stop whatever she is doing and come and watch you.

Stare at your daughter's food processor suspiciously. Ask her to help you operate it. Chop the carp in it for fifteen seconds, then move all the ingredients into your ancient wooden chopping bowl, which you lugged over just in case.

Get those Hadassah arms going: Attack the ingredients with a dull-bladed *hockmesser* for a good ninety minutes. Demand that your daughter acknowledge the superiority of your withered arm over that motorized gizmo.

Place your hand on your chest and moan. Accept your daughter's offer to help. Give her the bowl and the *hockmesser*.

Twelve seconds later, snatch the bowl and chopper out of your daughter's hands. Tell her to watch carefully so she'll be more of a help next year. Pulverize the fish with your chopper for at least another forty-five minutes.

On the bottom of a cast-iron pot with a nonmatching lid, arrange slices of carrots, onions, celery, fish heads, skin, and bones.

Form the chopped fish mush into oval patties and lay them gently on top of the ingredients in the pot.

Add liquid and seasonings, bring the pot to a boil, lower to simmer, cover the pot, and let the fish cook until they're ready and taste good—but not as good as last year's.

After the patties cool, arrange them on a beautiful serving platter for your daughter and her guests. Dump the heads, skin, and bones on a chipped plate for yourself. For a day or two beforehand, practice saying that the heads and the bones are the tastiest portions until you can sound convincing.

Two elderly Jewish grandmothers ran into each other at a Laundromat after not seeing each other for some time. After inquiring about each other's health, one asked how the other's husband was doing.

"Oh! Jake died last week. He went out to the garden to dig up a cabbage for dinner, had a heart attack, and dropped dead right there in the middle of the vegetable patch!"

"Oh dear! I'm very sorry," replied her friend. "What did you do?"

"Opened a can of peas instead."

A little old Jewish grandmother got onto a crowded bus and stood in front of a seated young girl. Holding her hand to her chest, she said to the girl, "If you knew what I have, you would give me your seat."

The girl got up and gave up her seat to the old lady.

It was a very hot day, and the bus was not air-conditioned. Presently, the girl pulled a fan from her purse and started fanning herself.

The woman looked up and said, "If you knew what I have, you would give me that fan."

With a sigh, the girl gave her the fan, too.

Fifteen minutes later, the woman got up and said to the bus driver, "Stop, I want to get off here."

The bus driver calmly told her he had to drop her at the next corner, not in the middle of the block.

With her hand across her chest, she told the driver, "If you knew what I have, you would let me off the bus right here."

The bus driver pulled over and opened the door to let her out. As she climbed out of the bus, he asked, "Madam, what is it you have?"

The old woman looks at him and replied with a cackle, "Chutzpah."

Sitting on the side of the highway waiting to catch speeding drivers, a State Police officer noticed a car puttering along at twenty-two miles per hour. He said to himself, "This driver is just as dangerous as a speeder!" So he turned on his lights and pulled the car over.

Approaching the vehicle, he noticed that there were five elderly ladies, eyes wide and white as ghosts. The driver, Grandma Phyllis Schechter, was obviously confused, "Officer," she said, "I don't understand, I was doing exactly the speed limit! What seems to be the problem?"

"Ma'am," the officer replied, "you weren't speeding, but you should know that driving slower than the speed limit can also be a danger to other drivers."

"Slower than the speed limit?" she asked. "No sir, I was doing the speed limit exactly: twenty-two miles an hour!" Bubbe says proudly.

The State Police officer, trying to contain a chuckle, explains to her that "22" was the route number, not the speed limit.

A bit embarrassed, she grinned and thanked the officer for pointing out her error.

The officer said, "But before I let you go, ma'am, I have to ask . . . is everyone in this car okay? These women seem awfully shaken, and they haven't muttered a single peep this whole time," the officer asked.

Bubbe replied, "Oh, they'll be all right in a minute officer. We just got off Route 119."

Two very elderly Jewish grandmothers were enjoying the sunshine on a park bench in Miami. They had been meeting at that park every sunny day for over twelve years, chatting and enjoying each other's friendship.

One day the younger of the two ladies turned to the other and said, "Please don't be angry with me, dear, but I am embarrassed, after all these years. . . . What is your name? I'm trying to remember, but I just can't."

The older friend stared at her, looking very distressed, said nothing for two full minutes, and finally with tearful eyes, said, "How soon do you have to know?"

An old Jewish grandmother attended an MPAA screening as a member of a focus group, to help determine what the movie's rating should be. She watched a remake of an old Roman Centurion movie. In the middle of the movie there was a scene where the Romans fed people to lions.

She pressed her buzzer and announced that the movie should be rated "R" because there were Jews getting fed to lions.

The focus group director said, "They're not Jews, they're Christians."

She said, "Okay."

The movie continued. A few minutes later she pressed the buzzer again. This time she said, "That lion over there is not eating!"

Three Jewish grandmothers were sitting around, drinking tea and talking about their grandsons' professions. One was a doctor, the second an architect, and the third a computer scientist. The grandmothers got to arguing about whose profession was the oldest.

In the course of their arguments, they got all the way back to the Garden of Eden, whereupon the doctor's grandma said, "The medical profession is clearly the oldest, because Eve was made from Adam's rib, as the story goes, and that was a simply incredible surgical feat."

The architect's grandmother did not agree. She said, "But if you look at the Garden itself, in the beginning there was chaos and void, and out of that, the Garden and the world were created. So God must have been an architect."

The computer scientist's grandmother, who had listened to all of this said, "Yes, but where do you think the chaos came from?"

*   *   *

A young Jewish mother was preparing a brisket one Friday for *Shabbos* dinner. Her daughter watched curiously as the mother sliced both ends off the brisket before placing it in the roasting pan.

The young girl asked her mother why she did this. The mother pauses for a moment, then said, "You know, I'm not sure. This is just the way I always saw my mother make a brisket. Let's call Grandma and ask her."

She telephoned the grandmother and asked why she always sliced the ends off the brisket before roasting. The grandmother thought for a moment and then admitted, "I'm not sure why, but this is the way I always saw *my* mother make a brisket."

Now the two women were very curious, so as soon as they could, they paid a visit to the great-grandmother in the nursing home. "You know when we make a brisket," they explained, "we always slice off the ends before roasting. Why is that?"

"I don't know why you do it," said the old woman, "but I did it because I never had a pan that was large enough!"

RABBIS

Humor in this chapter is certainly not restricted to rabbis as teachers and scholars. These jokes explore many corners of rabbis' personalities and attitudes, and in fact, rabbis emerge as perhaps the most multifaceted characters in this entire collection.

*   *   *

Matthew, a young Jewish boy, decided he really wanted to be an aeronautical engineer and build airplanes. He studied hard for ten years, went to the best schools, and finally got his degree. It didn't take long before he gained a reputation as the finest aeronautical engineer in all the land, so he decided to start his own company to build jets.

His company was such a hit that the president of the United States called Matthew into his office. "Matthew," the president said, "Israel wants to commission your company to build an advanced jet fighter for their country. You have our approval—go out and design the best jet fighter ever made."

Needless to say, Matthew was tremendously excited by this

prospect. The entire resources of his company went into building the most advanced jet fighter in history. Everything looked terrific on paper, but when they held the first test flight of the new jet, disaster struck. The wings couldn't take the strain—they broke clean off the fuselage! (Fortunately, the test pilot ejected and parachuted to safety.)

Matthew was devastated. His company redesigned the jet fighter, but the same thing happened during the next test flight—the wings broke clean off.

Beside himself with worry, Matthew went to his shul to pray, to ask God where he had gone wrong.

The rabbi saw Matthew's sadness, and naturally asked him what the matter was. Matthew decided to pour his heart out to the rabbi.

After hearing the problem with the jet fighter, the rabbi put his hand on Matthew's shoulder and told him, "Listen, Matthew, I know how to solve your problem. All you have to do is drill a row of holes directly above and below where the wing meets the fuselage. If you do this, I absolutely guarantee the wings won't fall off."

Matthew just smiled and thanked the rabbi for his advice. But the more he thought about it, the more he realized he had nothing to lose. And after all, maybe the rabbi had some holy insight. So Matthew did exactly what the rabbi told him to do.

On the next design of the jet fighter, he and his associates drilled a row of holes directly above and below where the wings met the fuselage. And it worked! The next test flight went perfectly!

Brimming with joy, Matthew went to shul to tell the rabbi that his advice had worked. "Naturally," said the rabbi, "I never doubted it would."

"But Rabbi, how did you know that drilling the holes would prevent the wings from falling off?"

"Matthew," the rabbi intoned, "I'm an old man. I've lived for many, many years and I've celebrated Passover many, many times. And in all those years, not once—*not once!*—has the matzoh broken on the perforation!"

Rabbi Feingold was an avid golfer and played as often as he could. In fact, he was so addicted to the game that if he didn't play he would actually get withdrawal symptoms.

One Yom Kippur, Rabbi Feingold wondered aloud, "Who is it going to hurt if during the recess I go out and play a few holes? Nobody will be the wiser and I'll be back in plenty of time for services."

Sure enough, at the conclusion of the Ma'ariv service, Rabbi Finkelstein snuck out of the synagogue and headed straight for the golf course.

Looking down upon him were one of the prophets and God.

The prophet said, "Look what that rabbi is doing!"

God replied, "I'll teach him a lesson."

On the course itself Rabbi Finkelstein teed off and when he hit the ball, it careened off a tree, struck a rock, flew across a stream, and landed in the hole for a *hole in one!*

Seeing all this, the prophet yelled, "God, how is this going to teach him a lesson? He got a hole in one!"

"Sure," said God, "but who can he tell?"

Max and Isaac came to the rabbi's study to settle a dispute. The rabbi's wife was also seated in the room.

Max explained his complaint to the rabbi: This and that happened, and he felt he had to do this and not that. He gave a fine account and argued his case eloquently.

After a few moments, the rabbi declared, "You're right, Max."

Next, Isaac presented his side. He spoke with such passion and persuasion that the rabbi said to him, "You're right, Isaac."

After they left, the rabbi's wife was distraught, and she said to her husband, "They have conflicting stories. How can you say that both of them are right? When one wins, the other must lose."

The rabbi thought long and hard and finally said to his wife, "You know, you're right."

A pious rabbi passed away and arrived in heaven; he was immediately served a meal of schmaltz herring. Though surprised and a little disappointed at this humble meal, the rabbi said nothing. But later, glimpsing into the Other Place, he noticed that people there were eating bagels and lox, toast, and eggs.

For the next meal the rabbi was again served a plate of schmaltz herring, only this time it was accompanied by a glass of tea. After the meal, the rabbi looked again at the Other Place, and noticed that the people there were feasting on blintzes, soup, sour cream, and berries.

For supper an angel came and brought the rabbi another plate of schmaltz herring and a glass of tea. Later, he looked at the Other Place, where he noticed that the people were eating steak and turkey, and drinking fine wine.

Finally, the rabbi could not control himself, and he turned to the angel and said, "I don't understand it. This is supposed to be heaven, but all I get to eat is schmaltz herring. But in the Other Place, I see that they eat like kings."

The angel gave an uneasy smile and replied, "I know. But to tell you the truth, it doesn't pay to cook for just two people."

An IRS official came to a rural synagogue for an inspection. The rabbi accompanied him around the synagogue.

"So Rabbi, tell me, please, after you have distributed all your unleavened bread, what do you do with the crumbs?"

"Why, we gather them carefully and send them to the city where they make bread with them and send it to us."

"Ah. So what about candles after they are burned? What do you do with the wax drippings?"

"We send them to the city as well, and they make new candles from them and send them to us."

"And what about circumcision? What do you do with those leftover pieces?"

The rabbi, wearily, replies, "We send them to the city as well."

"To the city?! And what do they send to you?"

"Today they have sent us you."

A rabbi retired and moved to the country to enjoy life and practice his hobby of gardening.

The day came when he needed a lawn mower, so he headed into town to buy one. On the way he saw a sign advertising a lawn mower for sale. He stopped at the house and a young lad came out to greet him. The rabbi asked about the lawn mower and the kid said it was behind the house.

The two went to look at the lawn mower. The engine was sputtering along at idle speed. The rabbi increased the speed of the engine and mowed a few strips. Satisfied that the mower would do the job they settled on a price of $25.

Later in the day the young lad was riding his bicycle when he spied the rabbi pulling on the engine starter cord.

The kid stopped and watched for a couple of minutes. He asked, "What's wrong?"

The reply came, "I can't get this mower started. Do you know how?"

The kid said, "Yep."

"Well, how do you do it? Tell me!" the rabbi yelled.

The kid replied, "You have to cuss it."

The rabbi rose up indignantly. "Now you listen here. I am a rabbi, and if I ever did cuss, and I'm not saying I have, I've forgotten how to do it after all these years."

With a wise look well beyond his years, the kid said, "Rabbi, you keep on pulling that cord and it'll all come back to you."

A passenger jet was suffering through a severe thunderstorm.

As the passengers were being bounced around by the turbulence, a young woman turned to her seatmate, a rabbi, and with a nervous laugh asked, "Rabbi, you're a man of God, can't you do something about this storm?"

He replied, "Lady, I'm in sales, not management."

The president of the congregation came to the rabbi. "Tell me, Rabbi," he asked, "why is it that a godly man like you is always talking about business? I'm a businessman myself, but once I leave my office, I talk about nothing but spiritual matters."

"This follows a very sound principle," replied the rabbi.

"And what principle is that, Rabbi?"

"Oh, the principle that people usually like to discuss things they know nothing about."

Four rabbis had an ongoing series of theological arguments, and three were always in accord against the fourth.

One day, after the usual "three-to-one, majority-rules" statement that meant he had lost again, the odd rabbi decided to appeal to a higher authority. "Oh, God!" he cried. "I know in my heart that I am right and they are wrong! Please give me a sign to prove it to them!"

It was a beautiful, sunny day, but the moment the rabbi finished his prayer, a storm cloud moved across the sky above the four. It rumbled once and dissolved.

"A sign from God!" cried the rabbi who had prayed. "See, I'm right, I knew it!"

But the other three disagreed, pointing out that storm clouds form on hot days.

So the rabbi prayed again: "Oh, God, I need a bigger sign to show that I am right and they are wrong. So please, God, a bigger sign!"

This time four storm clouds appeared, rushed toward one another to form one big cloud, and a bolt of lightning slammed into a tree on a nearby hill.

"I told you I was right!" cried the rabbi, but his friends insisted that nothing had happened that could not be explained by natural causes.

The rabbi was getting ready to ask for a "very big" sign, but just as he said "Oh God . . . ," the sky turned pitch-black, the earth shook, and a deep, booming voice intoned, *"Heeeeeeee's riiiiiiight!"*

The rabbi put his hands on his hips, turned to the other three, and said, "Well?"

"So," shrugged one of the other rabbis, "now it's three to two!"

A rabbi and his wife were doing a bit of house cleaning. The rabbi came across a box he didn't recognize. His wife told him to leave it alone, that it was personal.

One day when she was out, his curiosity got the best of him. He opened the box, and inside he found three eggs and $2,000.

When his wife came home, he admitted that he opened the box, and he asked her to explain the contents to him.

She told him that every time he gave a bad sermon, she would put an egg in the box.

He interrupted, "In twenty years, only three bad sermons, that's not bad."

His wife continued, "And every time I got a dozen eggs, I would sell them for one dollar."

There once were two evil brothers. They were rich and used their money to keep their evil ways from the public eye. They attended the same temple, and to everyone else they appeared to be perfect Jews.

One day, their rabbi retired and a new one was hired. Not only did the new rabbi see right through the brothers' deceptions, but he also spoke well and true about it. Because of the rabbi's honesty and integrity, the temple's membership grew in numbers. Eventually, a fund-raising campaign was started to build a much bigger temple.

All of a sudden, one of the brothers died. The remaining brother sought out the new rabbi the day before the funeral and handed him a check for the amount needed to complete the new building. He held the check for the rabbi to see.

"I have only one condition," he said. "At the funeral, you must say that my brother was a mensch. You must say those exact words."

After some thought, the rabbi gave his word and took the check. He cashed it immediately.

At the funeral the next day, however, the rabbi did not hold back. "He was an evil man," he said about the dead brother. "He cheated on his wife and abused his family. Never once did he commit an unselfish act." He railed on and on about the deceased.

After nearly a half hour of the evil truth, the rabbi paused and shrugged his shoulders. Finally, he said, "But compared to his brother, he was a mensch."

A couple preparing for a religious conversion to Judaism meets with the Orthodox rabbi for their last session.

The rabbi asks if they have any final questions.

The man asks, "Is it true that men and women don't dance together?"

"Yes," says the rabbi. "For modesty reasons, men and women dance separately."

"So I can't dance with my own wife?"

"No, definitely not."

"Well, okay," says the man, "but what about sex?"

"Fine," says the rabbi. "A mitzvah within the marriage."

"What about different positions?" the man asks.

"No problem," says the rabbi.

"Woman on top?" the man asks.

"Why not?" replies the rabbi.

"How about doggie-style?"

"Of course!"

"Well, what about standing up?"

"*No!*" says the rabbi.

"Why not?" asks the man.

"That could lead to dancing!"

After years and years of hard work, a man who has finally made his way in business decided to treat himself and buy an extravagance: a new Lamborghini.

However, after buying it, he felt a bit guilty. So he went to the rabbi of the Orthodox synagogue in his town and asks for a mezuzah (a parchment scroll placed over the doorway to bless a Jewish home) for the Lamborghini.

"You want a mezuzah for what?" the rabbi asked.

"It's a Lamborghini," the man replied.

"What's a Lamborghini?" asked the rabbi.

"A car, an Italian sports car."

"What? That is blasphemy!" the rabbi shouted. "You want a mezuzah for a sports car? Go to the Conservatives!"

The man was reluctant, but after a few days he finally went to the Conservative rabbi to ask for a mezuzah.

"You want a mezuzah for what?" the rabbi asked.

"It's a Lamborghini," the man replied.

"What's a Lamborghini?" asked the rabbi.

"A car, an Italian sports car."

"What? That is blasphemy!" the rabbi shouted. "You want a mezuzah for a sports car? Go to the Reformed!"

Again, the man felt guilty, but finally he broke down and went to the Reformed rabbi.

"Rabbi," he asked, "I'd like a mezuzah for my Lamborghini."

"You have a Lamborghini?" asks the rabbi.

"You know what it is?"

"Of course! It's a fantastic Italian sports car! Can I see it?"

They go out and the rabbi carefully looked over the entire car, finally settling into the driver's seat.

"Well, this is marvelous," the rabbi told the man. "I have only one question."

"What's that?"

"What's a mezuzah?"

There was a famous rabbi who could move any congregation to tears with his eloquence. One day he delivered the eulogy at the funeral of a prominent citizen. He elaborated on the life of the deceased with deeply touching verve, referring to the purity and generosity of his character, to the sheer nobility of his many good deeds, and to the insufferable tragedy of his sudden demise. Nonetheless, his listeners were unmoved. Not even the members of the man's immediate family shed a single tear.

One of the rabbi's admirers came up to him after the eulogy. "Rabbi, how is it you weren't able to wring a single tear out of the mourners?"

"My job is only to turn on the faucet," answered the rabbi. "It's not my fault if nothing comes out."

The results of a computerized survey indicated that the perfect rabbi preaches exactly fifteen minutes.

He condemns sins but never upsets anyone.

He works from eight A.M. until midnight and is also a janitor.

He makes $50 a week, wears good clothes, buys good books, drives a good car, and gives about $50 weekly to the poor.

He is twenty-eight years old and has preached thirty years.

He has a burning desire to work with teenagers and spends all his time with senior citizens.

The perfect rabbi smiles all the time with a straight face because he has a sense of humor that keeps him seriously dedicated to his work.

He makes fifteen calls daily on congregation families, shut-ins, and the hospitalized, and is always in his office when needed.

If your rabbi does not measure up, simply bundle up your rabbi and send him to the synagogue on the top of the attached list. Then add your synagogue address to the bottom of the list, delete the first synagogue on the list, and send this letter to six other synagogues that are tired of their rabbi, too, within three days. In less than two weeks, you will receive 1,296 rabbis and one of them will be perfect. Have faith in this procedure.

One congregation broke the chain and got its old rabbi back in less than three weeks . . . so don't break the chain.

*   *   *

The rabbi rose before his congregation with a red face. "Someone in this congregation has spread a rumor that I belong to the K.K.K. This is a horrible lie and one that a Jewish community cannot tolerate! I am embarrassed and do not intend to accept this. Now, I want the party who did this to stand and ask forgiveness from God and our Jewish community."

No one moved.

The rabbi continued, "Do you not have the nerve to face me and admit this is a falsehood? Remember, you will be forgiven and in your heart you will feel relief. Now stand and confess your transgression!"

Again all was quiet. Slowly a gorgeous blonde in the third pew rose to her feet. Her head was bowed, and her voice quivered as she spoke. "Rabbi," she said, "there has been a terrible misunderstanding. I never said you were a member of the Ku Klux Klan. I just told a couple of friends that you were a wizard under the sheets."

A Jewish father was very troubled by the way his son turned out, and went to see his rabbi about it. "I brought him up in the faith, gave him a very expensive bar mitzvah, cost me a fortune to educate him. Then he tells me last week he has decided to be a Christian! Rabbi, where did I go wrong?"

"Funny you should come to me," said the rabbi. "Like you, I, too, brought my boy up in the faith, put him through university, cost me a fortune, then one day he, too, tells me he has decided to become a Christian."

"What did you do?" asked the troubled father.

"I turned to God for the answer," replied the rabbi.

"And what did he say?" pressed the father.

"He said, 'Funny you should come to me. . . .'"

Three Reform rabbis were in a terrible car accident. None survived. One minute they were driving along the highway, talking and laughing and joking, and the next, *boom!* they found themselves before the Creator of all.

Shaking his head, the Omnipotent One looks at the three.

"Reform I can understand. But where will it end? You! Goldblum! The ashtrays in your temple so my people could smoke while the Torah was being read?"

Goldblum shuddered.

God went on. "I can live with that. Men are weak, but the Word is strong!"

Goldblum sighed with relief.

"Bauman! I can certainly accept that my people need to eat, but really: Ham and cheese sandwiches at the temple during Yom Kippur?"

Bauman hung his head in shame.

"Even that I can allow to pass, even with the eating of that which is not kosher. I'm not pleased at all with playing fast and loose with my people, but I can accept these indiscretions."

Bauman also heaved a sigh of relief.

Finally, He turned to the third rabbi and said, "You, Rabinowitz, have gone too far! Am I asking too much? No, you flaunt the world at me, even on the holiest days of Rosh Hashanah and Yom Kippur by putting out a sign that says, 'Closed for the Holidays!'"

A rich man and a poor man sat in the waiting room of an eminent rabbi's office. The rich man was let in first and remained in consultation for over an hour. When the poor man finally went into the rabbi's private chambers, he was given only a few minutes of consultation.

"Rebbe," said the poor man as he was ushered from the room, "are you not discriminating between rich men and poor men?"

The rabbi looked reproachfully at the man. "Foolish fellow!" he declared. "When you came in I knew immediately from looking at you that you were a poor man, but I had to talk with the other one for an hour before I found out he was as poor as you are!"

A minister, a priest, and a rabbi went for a hike one day. It was very hot. They were sweating and exhausted by the time they came upon a small lake. Since it was fairly secluded, they took off all their clothes and jumped in the water.

Feeling refreshed, the trio decided to pick a few berries while enjoying their "freedom." As they were crossing an open area, who should come along but a group of ladies from town.

Unable to get to their clothes in time, the minister and the priest covered their privates and the rabbi covered his face while they ran for cover.

After the ladies had left and the men got their clothes back on, the minister and the priest asked the rabbi why he covered his face rather than his privates.

The rabbi replied, "I don't know about you, but in *my* congregation, it's my face they would recognize."

There was a young couple that was very much in love. On the eve of the day they were to be married, both were tragically killed in an automobile accident. They found themselves at the gates of heaven being escorted in by an angel.

After a couple of weeks in heaven, the prospective groom took the angel aside and said, "Listen, my fiancée and I are very happy to be in heaven but we miss very much the opportunity to have celebrated our wedding vows. Is it possible for people in heaven to get married?"

The angel looked at him and said, "I'm sorry, I've never heard of anyone in heaven wanting to get married. I'm afraid you'll have to talk to the Almighty about that. I can get you an appointment for two weeks from Wednesday."

On the appointed day, the couple was escorted by guardian angels into the presence of God, where they humbly repeated the request.

The Lord looked at them solemnly and said, "I'll tell you what, wait five years, and if you still want to get married, come back and we will talk about it again."

Five years went by, and the couple still very much wanted to get married, so they returned to God. Again the Lord God Almighty said, "Please, you must wait another five years and then I will consider your request."

Finally, they come before Hashem a third time, ten years after their first request, and ask the Lord again. This time the Lord answered, "Yes, you may marry. This Saturday at two P.M., we will have a beautiful service in the main sanctuary. The reception will be on me!"

The wedding went beautifully, all the guests thought the bride looked beautiful, and the reception was spectacular.

But after just a few weeks, the couple realized that they had made a horrible mistake, that they just couldn't stay married to each other.

So they made another appointment to see the Hashem, this time to ask if they could get a divorce in heaven.

When the Lord heard their request, he looked at them sternly and said, "Look, it took us ten years to find a rabbi up here in heaven. Do you have any idea how long it'll take to find a lawyer?"

Long ago in a Polish town there lived a wise rabbi. One night a peddler came to the rabbi's house. "Rabbi," he said, "I am going to kill myself!"

"Heaven, forbid!" cried the rabbi. "What could make you have such a sinful thought?"

"Is it better that I should starve to death! Today my horse died and without a horse I cannot earn my living!"

"Look," said the rabbi, "the Holy One, Blessed be He, will provide for you. Tonight, at midnight, meet me at the stable of the Count."

The peddler had no idea what the rabbi could mean, but obediently he arrived at the Count's stables at exactly midnight. The rabbi took him to one of the stalls and told him to take the beautiful white stallion standing there.

"*Oy vay!*" said the peddler, "I can't do this, the Count will have me hanged!"

"Don't worry," the rabbi assured him, "take the horse and go in peace." In those days, one did not disobey a rabbi, so the peddler did as he was told.

When he had gone the rabbi lay down in the stall and went to sleep. The next morning the Count arrived with his groom, and seeing the man asleep on the floor, kicked him and cried: "Hey you, who are you, what are you doing here, where's my horse?!"

The rabbi sat up and rubbed his eyes. Then he jumped to his feet and raised his hands to the sky and cried: "Thanks be to God, creator of the Universe!"

"What's this, what's this," cried the Count. "What is going on, who are you, where is my horse?"

"Don't you understand?" said the rabbi, "I was your horse!

I used to be a famous scholar. But one night I succumbed to the Evil Impulse and stole money. In punishment the Holy One turned me into your horse. But in my misery I repented and prayed for forgiveness. Finally my prayers were heard and I have been changed back into a human being. Thanks be to God, creator of the Universe!"

Now the Count was a devout man and a respecter of miracles and so he also cried, "Thanks be to God, creator of the Universe!" and let the rabbi go.

Several weeks later the Count was riding through the town. Suddenly he spied the peddler leading his beautiful white stallion. He leaped from his carriage and ran to the beast, struck him brutally on the rear end with his riding crop and shrieked: "Scoundrel! Ingrate! Stealing again?!"

A rabbi was invited to address the inmates of an insane asylum. Upon his arrival, the warden explained to him what he could expect to encounter. "Please pay no attention to any comments made during your address."

The rabbi spoke for about a half hour, and things had been going along without incident when all of a sudden one of the inmates leaped to his feet and began screaming, "Good Lord! This is terrible! I can't stand it!" With that, he rushed into the aisle and left the auditorium.

The rabbi, a little shaken, nevertheless continued, and when he had finished, the warden came up to thank him warmly. "It was so nice of you to come today, Rabbi, and you've done a world of good!"

"Thank you," the rabbi replied dubiously, "but I certainly hope I didn't upset that fellow too much."

"On the contrary!" said the warden. "You helped him most of all. That was the first rational sentence he's uttered in six years."

JEWS AND NON-JEWS

*F*or a number of obvious reasons, to Jews, humor about non-Jews is perhaps the most important—and funniest—of all. It is here that the notion of humor-as-defense-mechanism is made most prominently manifest. These jokes will be funniest to anyone, Jewish or non-Jewish, who has ever truly felt like an outsider.

*   *   *

An elderly Jew was on his deathbed and, much to the astonishment of his relatives, he sent for a priest.

When the priest arrived, the man declared, "I want to convert."

Confused, the priest asked, "Sir, why on earth would you want to become a Catholic when you've lived all your life a Jew?"

"Better one of them should die than one of us!" the man snapped.

At a mass at which some young women were to take their final vows to become nuns, the presiding bishop noticed two rabbis enter the church just before the mass began.

They insisted on sitting on the right side of the center aisle at the back of the sanctuary.

The bishop wondered why they had come, but didn't have time to inquire before the mass began. When the time came for some announcements, his curiosity got the best of him. He announced that he was delighted to see two rabbis in their midst at the mass, but was curious as to why they were present at this occasion, where the young women were to become the "brides of Christ."

The eldest of the rabbis slowly rose to his feet and explained, "We are family of the groom."

A little boy climbed up onto the lap of a department-store Santa Claus and was promptly asked what he wanted for Christmas.

"Nothing," the lad answered. "We celebrate Hanukkah."

"I see," said Santa. "Then, what would you like for Hanukkah?"

"A Christmas tree," the boy replied.

Two seven-year-olds were playing in a school yard. One is Jewish, the other is Catholic. The Catholic boy said to the Jewish boy, "Our priest knows more than your rabbi!"

To which the Jewish boy replied, "Of course he does, you tell him everything."

Back in the 1920s, Rivkah Green from Denver decided to go on vacation to Miami. Upon arriving she attempted to check her baggage and settle into a quality hotel.

The concierge told her, "Sorry, there's no vacancy."

Just then, a man and his wife suddenly checked out.

Rivkah exclaimed, "Thank God! You now have a room."

"Sorry," the man behind the counter replied, "this hotel is restricted."

"And what does that mean?" she asked him.

"Jews aren't allowed here!"

"Well, what makes you think I'm Jewish?" Rivkah shot back.

"I know you are!"

"Well, I'm not! I'm a Catholic!" she insisted.

"Oh, really? So tell me," the man replied, "did God have a son?"

"Sure."

"What was his name?"

"Jesus."

"And where was he born?"

"In Bethlehem, in a stable."

"And *why* was he born there?"

"Because a shmuck like you wouldn't rent his Jewish parents a room!"

Two beggars were sitting on a park bench in Mexico City. One held a crucifix and the other a Star of David. Both held hats to collect contributions.

People walked by, lifted their noses at the man with the Star of David, and dropped money in the hat held by the man with the crucifix.

Soon the hat of the man with the cross was filled to overflowing, while the hat of the man with the Star of David was completely empty.

A priest walking by noticed the men and approached them. He said to the man with the Star of David, "Young man. Don't you realize that this is a Catholic country? You'll never get any contributions in this country holding a Star of David."

The man with the Star of David turned to the beggar with the cross and said, "Moishe, can you imagine, this ditz is trying to tell us how to run our business?"

A Jewish family invited their Gentile neighbor for holiday dinner. The first course was set in front of him, and when he looked puzzled, the Jewish couple explained, "This is matzoh ball soup."

On seeing the two large matzoh balls in the soup, the Gentile man was hesitant to taste this strange-looking brew. Gently, the Jewish couple pressed the Gentile man. "Just have a taste. If you don't like it, you don't have to finish it."

Finally he agreed. He gingerly sliced off a tiny nibble of the matzoh ball with his spoon, and tasted it carefully. He was so pleased that he quickly finished the soup.

"That was delicious," he said. "Say, can you eat any other parts of the matzoh?"

Four people were in the final stages of interviewing for a very prestigious job. One was Christian, one was Catholic, one was a Buddhist, and the fourth was Jewish.

The company decided to fly them all in for dinner and a final interview.

Over dinner at a fine restaurant, the president of the company told them that all were very worthy applicants, and that he wished he could hire them all, but they had only enough money budgeted to hire one person. He told them that he would call each of them in one at a time for a final interview the next day, and that he would ask each one of them the same question. Whoever gave the best answer to the question would be the one hired. The applicants all agreed that this was fair.

The next day the first applicant, the Christian, was called in. The president posed the question, "What is the fastest thing in the world?"

He thought for a moment and replied, "That would have to be a thought."

"Why do you say that?" asked the president.

"Well, a thought takes no time at all. It is in your mind in an instant, then gone again."

"Ahh, very good. Thank you," replied the president.

Next, the same question was posed to the Catholic woman. "What is the fastest thing in the world?"

She paused and replied, "That would have to be a blink."

"And why?" asked the president.

"Because you don't even think about a blink, it's just a reflex. You do it in an instant."

The president thanked her, then called in the next person.

The Buddhist was asked what the fastest thing in the world was, and after hesitating for a brief moment, he replied, "I would have to say electricity."

"Why?"

Because a man can flip a switch, and immediately, three miles away a light will go on."

"I see, very good," replied the president.

Then the Jewish man was called in.

He, too, was asked, "What is the fastest thing in the world?"

"That's easy . . . " he replied, "that would have to be diarrhea!"

Rather stunned, the president asked, "Why do you say that?"

"Well, last night after dinner, I was lying in my bed and I got the worst case of stomach cramps, and before I could *think, blink,* or *turn on the lights* . . . "

He got the job.

A rabbi and a minister were playing a game of golf. They decided to play for $5 a hole.

On the third hole, the minister hit his ball into the rough. "Help me find my ball," the minister said to the rabbi. "You look over there."

After several minutes, neither had any luck, and, anxious to win, the minister pulled out another ball and dropped it on the ground. "I've found my ball!" he announced.

The rabbi looked at him, "After all the years we've been friends, you'd cheat me at golf for a measly five bucks?"

"Cheat? I found my ball right here!"

"And a liar, too!" the rabbi said with amazement. "I'll have you know I've been standing on your ball since we got here."

Two old Jewish men were strolling down the street one day, when they happened to walk by a Catholic church.

Above the door of the church they saw a big sign that said, "Convert to Catholicism and get $10."

One of the Jewish men stopped walking and stared at the sign. His friend turned to him and said, "Murray, what's going on?"

"Abe," replied Murray, "I'm thinking of doing it."

Abe said, "What are you, crazy?!"

Murray thought for a minute and said, "Abe, I'm going to do it."

With that, Murray strode purposefully into the church.

Twenty minutes later, he came out of the church with his head bowed.

"So," asks Abe, "did you get your ten dollars?"

Murray looked up at him and snapped, "Is that all you people think about?"

The rabbi and the priest met each and every Sunday at two P.M. in the park to talk over the week's events. They rode their bicycles to a special bench every Sunday for twenty years.

One Sunday the rabbi arrived at their bench precisely at two and waited and waited. An hour went by and the priest was still not there.

The rabbi rode home and called the priest on the phone. "Hey, Father, what happened? For twenty years we've met at the park every Sunday but today you didn't show up. What's wrong?"

"Well, Rabbi," the priest explained, "after church today I went out to get my bike to meet you, but my bike was missing. I know it must have been someone in my parish who took it. Rabbi, what should I do?"

"Well, that's quite a dilemma, Father," the rabbi said thoughtfully. "I'll tell you what you should do. Next Sunday when you give your sermon, speak of the Ten Commandments. When you get to the part about 'Thou Shall Not Steal,' look over your congregation and the person with the guilty look will be the one who stole your bicycle."

The following Sunday at two the rabbi was already waiting for the priest.

Promptly at two up rode the priest on his bike.

"Well, Father, my idea must have worked," the rabbi smiled.

"Well, not quite," the priest replied. "I was going through the Ten Commandments as you suggested. But when I got to the part about 'Thou shalt not commit adultery,' I remembered where I left my bike."

A young Jewish boy from New York went out west to college. One day in his senior year he called home and said to his mother, "Mom. I've got a surprise for you. I'm getting married."

"Lucky you," his mom said. "Finding a nice young Jewish girl out in a place like Wyoming."

"Mom," his son replied, "she isn't Jewish. She's a Native American."

The mother fainted and wouldn't talk to him for a month.

When she finally agreed to come to the phone, she said, "If you're going to marry an Indian, at least bring her home to me."

Her son said, "Mom, we're already decided where to live. We're moving to the reservation."

The mother fainted again. This time she didn't talk to her son for six months.

When she finally agreed to come to the phone, her son said, "Mom, I've got some good news this time. You're going to be a grandmother."

She hesitated, then said, "A grandmother is not a bad thing to be." Feeling pleased for the first time, she called once a month to find out how things were coming along. Then one day she heard from her son. "Mom, I've got great news. We've just had a son. And we've decided to give him a Jewish name."

The mother smiled. "Ahh. A Jewish name for my grandson. What is it?"

"Smoked Whitefish."

A well-off southern woman living near an army base in Mississippi wanted to do something patriotic for the boys in uniform, so she decided to invite five officers to a party to meet the local girls.

She called the base and asked to speak to the general in charge. Excitedly she got right to the point, and invited five officers to a party to meet the local girls. But she added, "Don't send any Jews!"

The general agreed, "Okay."

The party was just getting under way the following weekend when there came a knock on the southern woman's door. When she opened the door, there stood five handsome *black* army officers.

"There must be some mistake," she muttered.

"No ma'am," answered the black captain. "General Cohen never makes mistakes!"

A rabbi, a priest, and a minister were out fishing in the middle of a lake. The priest told his two colleagues, "I forgot my fishing pole in the car; I'll be right back." He got out of the boat, walked across the water all the way to the beach, went to the car, retrieved his fishing pole, walked back across the lake, and got into the boat.

The rabbi stared in amazement.

A half hour later, the minister said, "I need to use the bathroom." He, too, got out of the boat, walked across the water, found the nearest men's room, and walked back across the water, and got into the boat.

The rabbi was absolutely dumbfounded! He kept thinking, "My faith is as great as theirs!" So he told the other two, "I need to get something to drink; there's a refreshment stand up on the beach." He stood up, put his feet on the water, and *splash!* went straight down under the water. When he bobbed back up to the surface, the priest and minister helped him back into the boat.

The rabbi was embarrassed, not to mention wet, but he knew he could do it if the other two could. So he stood up again, stepped out onto the water, and again, *splash!* When he came up again sputtering, the other two dragged him onto the boat.

He decided to try yet again. As he went down for the third time, the priest turned to the minister and asked, "Do you think we should show him where the rocks are?"

A rabbi and a minister decided to buy a new car together. The day after they bought it, the rabbi found the minister driving it. The minister explained that he had just gone to the car wash because, in his religion, it was customary to welcome a new member with the rite of baptism.

The next day, the minister discovered the rabbi cutting the end off the tailpipe.

A priest and a rabbi found themselves sharing a compartment on a train. After a while, the priest put down his book and opened a conversation by saying, "I know that, in your religion, you're not supposed to eat pork . . . but have you really never even tasted it?"

The rabbi closed his newspaper and responded, "I must tell you the truth. Yes I have, on the odd occasion."

The rabbi had his turn of interrogation. He asked, "I know that, in your religion, you're supposed to be celibate . . . but . . . "

The priest interjected, "Yes, I know what you are going to ask, and yes, I have succumbed to temptation once or twice."

The two resumed their reading. There was silence for a while.

Then the rabbi peeked around his newspaper and said, "Better than pork, isn't it?"

A rabbi and a priest got into a bad car accident. Both cars were totally demolished, but amazingly neither man was hurt.

After they crawled out of their wrecks, the rabbi noticed the priest's collar and said, "So you're a priest. I'm a rabbi. Just look at our cars. There's nothing left, but we are unhurt. This must be a sign from God. God must have meant that we should meet and be friends and live together in peace the rest of our days."

The priest replied, "I agree with you completely. This must be a sign from God."

The rabbi continued, "And look at this: Here's another miracle. My car is completely demolished but this bottle of Kedem wine didn't break. Surely God wants us to drink this wine and celebrate our good fortune."

He handed the bottle to the priest. The priest agreed and took a few big swigs. He handed the bottle back to the rabbi, who immediately clamped the cap back onto the bottle and handed it back to the priest.

The priest asked, "Aren't you having any?"

"No," the rabbi replied, "I think I'll wait for the police."

An old Jewish man was riding the subway sitting next to a younger man. He noticed that the young man had a strange kind of shirt collar. Having never seen a priest before, he asked the man, "Excuse me, sir, but why do you have your shirt collar on backwards?"

The priest was a bit flustered but politely answered, "I wear this collar because I am a Father."

The Jewish man thought for a moment and responded, "Sir, I am also a father but I wear my collar front-ways. Why do you wear your collar so differently?"

The priest thought for a minute and said, "Sir, I am the Father for many."

The Jewish man quickly answered, "I, too, am the father of many. I have four sons, four daughters, and too many grandchildren to count. But I wear my collar like everyone else does. I still want to know: Why do you wear it your way?"

The priest, exasperated, then blurted out, "Sir, I am the Father for hundreds and hundreds of people."

The Jewish man was taken aback and was silent for a long time. The train came to his stop. As he got up to leave the car, he leaned over to the priest and said, "Mister, maybe you should wear your pants backwards."

Sometime in the 1970s, a shipment of meat arrived in a town in the Soviet Union. The townspeople dutifully lined up at the town store to wait to be given their rations.

After about an hour, a man came out of the store and announced, "Comrades, I'm sorry to tell you, but there isn't enough meat for everyone, so the Jews have to leave."

The Jews in the line departed, grumbling.

About an hour later, the man came out of the store again and announced, "Comrades, I'm sorry to tell you this, but there isn't enough meat for everyone, so anyone who is not a member of the Communist Party will have to leave."

More grumbling as the non-Party members departed.

Another hour went by and the man came out of the store yet again and announced, "Comrades, I'm sorry to tell you this, but there isn't enough meat for everyone in the line, so anyone who wasn't a member of the Party before 1956 has to leave."

More grumbling as all the younger Party members left.

A few old people remained in the line.

Another hour passed. It was getting dark and it was cold. The same man emerged from the store and announced, "Comrades, I'm sorry to tell you this, but there isn't any meat. Go home."

One old lady in the line turned to her neighbor and says, "See? It's like I told you. The Jews always get the best treatment!"

A man was hit by a bus on a busy street in midtown Manhattan. He lay dying on the sidewalk as a crowd of spectators gathered around.

"A priest. Somebody get me a priest!" the man gasped.

A policeman checks the crowd—no priest, no minister, no man of God of any kind.

"Priest! A priest!" the dying man cried again.

Then out of the crowd stepped a little old Jewish man of at least eighty years of age. "Mr. Policeman," said the man, "I'm not a priest. I'm not even a Catholic. But for fifty years now I'm living behind St. Elizabeth's Catholic Church on First Avenue, and every night I'm listening to the Catholic litany. Maybe I can be of some comfort to this man."

The policeman agreed and brought the octogenarian over to the dying man. He knelt down, leaned over the injured man, and said in a solemn voice: "B-4. I-19. N-38. G-54. O-72. . . . "

Two nuns were discussing their travel plans.

"Where should I go on vacation?" the first nun asked the other.

"Go to Israel," said the second nun.

"No. There are too many Jews there," said the first nun.

"Well, go to New York, then."

"No," said the second nun, "there are too many Jews there!"

"How about Miami?" asked the first nun.

Once again the second nun replied, "No. There are two many Jews there."

A Jewish lady who had been sitting nearby heard the whole conversation and replied: "Go to hell. There are no Jews there!"

Three construction contractors died and went to heaven—a black, a Jew, and an Italian. When they got there Saint Peter welcomed them warmly and asked if they could do him a favor before they entered heaven. It seems that the Pearly Gates were in need of some repair, and he wanted some estimates.

The black contractor looked the job over carefully and estimated the job at $600. When asked how he came up with that figure, he said, "Two hundred materials, two hundred labor, and two hundred profit."

Saint Peter then asked the Jewish contractor for an estimate. After careful inspection the Jew answered, "Three thousand dollars—one thousand materials, one thousand labor, and one thousand profit."

When Saint Peter ask the Italian for an estimate, he answered immediately without looking over the job at all—$2600. Asked how he came up with that figure he answered, "Simple, one thousand for you, one thousand for me, and six hundred to get the low bidder over there to do the work."

A priest was called away for an emergency. Not wanting to leave the confessional unattended, he called his rabbi friend from across the street and asked him to cover for him. The rabbi told him he wouldn't know what to say, but the priest told him to come on over and he'd stay with him for a little bit and show him what to do.

So the rabbi went and he and the priest sat together in the receiving end of the confessional.

A few minutes later a woman came in and said, "Father, forgive me for I have sinned."

The priest asked, "What did you do?"

The woman said, "I committed adultery."

Priest: "How many times?"

Woman: "Three times."

Priest: "Say two Hail Marys, put five dollars in the box, and go and sin no more."

A few minutes later a man entered the confessional. He began as usual, "Father, forgive me for I have sinned."

Priest: "What did you do?"

Man: "I committed adultery."

Priest: "How many times?"

Man: "Three times."

Priest: "Say two Hail Marys, put five dollars in the box, and go and sin no more."

The rabbi told the priest that he thought he got the picture, so the priest left hurriedly to tend to the emergency.

A few minutes later another woman entered the confessional and said, "Father, forgive me for I have sinned."

Rabbi: "What did you do?"

Woman: "I committed adultery."

Rabbi: "How many times?"

Woman: "Once."

Rabbi: "Go do it two more times. We have a special this week, three for five dollars."

The main course at a big civic dinner was baked ham with glazed sweet potatoes. Rabbi Cohen regretfully shook his head when the platter was passed to him.

Father Kelly, sitting next to Rabbi Cohen, scolded him playfully. "When are you going to forget that silly rule of yours and enjoy ham like the rest of us?"

Without missing a beat, Rabbi Cohen replied, "At your wedding reception, Father Kelly."

God was tired, feeling completely worn out.

He went to Saint Peter. "You know," God said, "I need a vacation. Got any suggestions where I should go?"

Saint Peter thought for a moment. "Say, how about Jupiter? It's nice and warm there this time of the year."

God shook His head before saying, "No. Too much gravity. You know how that hurts my back."

"Hmmm," Saint Peter reflected. "Well, how about Mercury?"

"No way!" God muttered. "It's way too hot for me there!"

"I've got it!" Saint Peter said, his face lighting up. "How about going down to Earth for your vacation?"

God chuckled, "Are you kidding? Two thousand years ago I went there, had an affair with some nice Jewish girl, and they're *still* talking about it!"

A Jewish man went into a bar to have a drink. After a few drinks, a Chinese man came in and sat down next to him at the bar. The Jewish man immediately turned and punched the other man in the face.

The Chinese man shouted, "Hey! What was that for?"

The Jewish man replied, "That's for Pearl Harbor."

The Chinese man said, "You idiot, I'm Chinese, not Japanese!"

The Jewish man replied, "Chinese, Japanese, what's the difference?"

The Chinese man proceeded to punch the Jewish man in the face.

The Jewish man clutched his jaw and said angrily, "Owww, why did you do that?!"

The Chinese man replied, "That's for the *Titanic*."

The Jewish man said, "But an iceberg caused it to sink, not me!"

The Chinese man smiled and said, "Iceberg, Goldberg, what's the difference!"

A man was in the hospital recovering from an operation. One day a nun came into his room. She was making the rounds mainly to cheer up the patients. The man and the nun started talking and she asked about his life. He talked about his wife and thirteen children.

"My, my," said the nun, "thirteen children . . . why, you're a good, proper Catholic family. I'm sure God is very proud of you!"

"I'm sorry, sister," he said, "I'm not Catholic. I'm Jewish."

"Jewish?!" she replied and immediately got up to leave.

"Sister, why are you leaving?"

"I didn't realize I was talking to a sex maniac!"

*　　*　　*

A little old Jewish lady boarded a bus and sat down next to a young man. She looked him over for a few minutes and then asked, "Young man, are you Jewish?"

He replied, "No lady, I'm not Jewish."

She continued looking at him, and then asked again, "Are you Jewish?"

And again the man replied, "No lady, I'm not Jewish."

She kept watching him, and then again asked, "Are you sure you're not Jewish?"

The man was getting frustrated, and this time, to appease her, he said, "Yes, lady, I'm Jewish!"

"That's funny," she replied, "you don't look Jewish!!"

The chief rabbi of Israel and the pope had a meeting in Rome. The rabbi noticed an unusually fancy phone on a side table in the pope's private chambers. "What is that phone for?" he asked the pontiff.

"It's my direct line to the Lord."

The pope saw that the rabbi was skeptical, so he insisted that the rabbi try it out, and indeed, he was connected directly to the Lord. The rabbi held a lengthy discussion with Him.

After hanging up the rabbi said, "Thank you very much. This is great! But listen, I want to pay for my phone charges."

The pope, of course, refused, but the rabbi was steadfast and finally the pontiff gave in. He checked the counter on the phone and said, "All right! The charges were 100,000 liras" ($56). The chief rabbi gladly handed over the payment.

A few months later, the pope was in Jerusalem on an official visit. In the chief rabbi's chambers, he saw a phone identical to his and learned it was also a direct line to the Lord.

The pope remembered he had an urgent matter that required divine consultation, so he asked if he could use the rabbi's phone. The rabbi gladly agreed, handed him the phone, and the pope chatted away for a half hour.

After hanging up, the pope offered to pay in turn for the phone charges. Of course, the chief rabbi refused to accept payment. After the pope insisted, the rabbi relented and looked on the phone counter: "Shekel 50" (42 cents).

The pope looked surprised, "Why so cheap?"

The rabbi smiled, "Local call."

One day a Catholic priest goes to a barber for a haircut. After the haircut, he asks the barber how much he owes. The barber says, "For a man of the cloth, the haircut is free!"

The priest thinks, "What a nice man!" The next day the barber finds a case of wine outside his shop.

Then a minister comes in for a haircut. Again, the barber tells him that the haircut is free. The minister thinks, "What a nice man!" The next day, the barber finds a box of chocolates outside his shop.

Then a rabbi comes in for a haircut. Again, the barber gives the haircut on the house. The rabbi thinks, "What a nice man!" The next day, the barber finds a long line of rabbis outside his shop!

Proof That Jesus Was Jewish

He went into his father's business.

He lived at home until the age of thirty-three.

He was sure that his mother was a virgin, and his mother was sure that he was God.

A Jewish family had settled in a small New England town, and as the years went by, they became thoroughly assimilated.

In most ways they could hardly be told apart from their Christian neighbors. At Yuletide they always had a Christmas tree for their little boy who was as delighted with it as any other child in town.

One Christmas, when the boy was six, he was invited to a party given by a Gentile playmate. When he got home from the party he was filled with curiosity.

"Tell me, Dad," he asked, "do Gentiles, too, believe in Christmas?"

A century or two ago, the pope decided that all the Jews had to leave the Vatican. Naturally there was a considerable uproar from the Jewish community.

So the pope made a deal. He agreed to have a religious debate with a member of the Jewish community. If the Jew won, all the Jews could stay. If the pope won, the Jews would have to leave.

The Jews realized that they had no choice. So they picked a middle-aged man named Moishe to represent them.

Moishe asked for one addition to the debate. To make it more interesting, neither side would be allowed to talk. The pope agreed.

The day of the great debate came. Moishe and the pope sat opposite each other for a full minute before the pope raised his hand and showed three fingers. Moishe looked back at him and raised one finger. The pope waved his fingers in a circle around his head. Moishe pointed to the ground where he sat. The pope pulled out a wafer and a glass of wine. Moishe pulled out an apple. The pope stood up and said, "I give up. This man is too good. The Jews can stay."

An hour later the cardinals were all gathered around the pope asking him what happened. The pope said, "First I held up three fingers to represent the Trinity. He responded by holding up one finger to remind me that there was still one God common to both our religions. Then I waved my finger around me to show him that God was all around us. He responded by pointing to the ground, showing that God was also right here with us. I pulled out the wine and the wafer to show that God absolves us from our sins. He pulled out an apple to remind me of original sin. He had an answer for everything. What could I do?"

Meanwhile, the Jewish community had crowded around Moishe.

"What happened?" they asked.

"Well," said Moishe, "first he said to me that the Jews had three days to get out of here. I told him that not one of us was leaving. Then he told me that this whole city would be cleared of Jews. I let him know that we were staying right here."

"And then?" asked a woman.

"I don't know," said Moishe. "He took out his lunch and I took out mine."

A Catholic priest, a Protestant minister, and a rabbi were discussing what they would like people to say after they died and their bodies were on display in open caskets.

The priest said, "I would like someone to say, 'He was a righteous man, an honest man, and very generous.'"

The minister wanted someone to say, "He was very fair and kind, and he was very good to his parishioners."

The rabbi said, "I would want someone to say, 'Oh look! He's moving!'"

A Jew and a Christian were arguing about the relative merits of their religions.

The Jewish man insisted, "You people have been taking things from us for thousands of years. The Ten Commandments, for instance."

The Christian replied, "Well, it's true that we took the Ten Commandments from you, but you can't actually say that we've ever kept them."

*　　*　　*

A Jewish family was visiting a Catholic family at their summer resort. The little Jewish boy and the young Catholic girl decided to go for a swim in a stream out in the woods. Since they didn't have their bathing suits with them, they decided to "skinny-dip."

After swimming for a while, they took a rest on the bank. The girl couldn't help but notice their anatomical differences and said, "Gee, I didn't know there was such a difference between Catholics and Jews!"

An old man went into a confession booth and told the priest, "Father, I'm eighty years old, married, have four kids and eleven grandchildren, and last night I had an affair and I made love to two eighteen-year-old girls. Both of them. Twice."

The priest said, "Well, my son, when was the last time you came to confession?"

"Never, Father, I'm Jewish."

"So then, why are you telling me?"

"I'm telling everybody!"

There once was a businessman whose son proposed to a *shiksa*. The businessman warned his son against ever marrying outside his faith.

The son replied, "But Dad, she's converting to Judaism."

"It doesn't matter," the old man said. "A *shiksa* will cause problems."

After the wedding, the father called his son, who was in business with him, and asked him why he wasn't at work.

"It's *Shabbos,*" the son replied.

The father was surprised: "But we always work on Saturday. It's our busiest day."

"I won't work anymore on Saturday," the son insisted, "because my wife wants us to go to synagogue on *Shabbos.*"

"See?" the father said. "I told you marrying a *shiksa* would cause problems!"

Two elderly Jewish men were sitting in a Lower East Side deli frequented almost exclusively by Jews in New York City. As was their custom, they were conversing in Yiddish.

A Chinese waiter, only one year in New York, approached their table and in fluent impeccable Yiddish asked them if everything was okay and if they were enjoying the holiday.

The Jewish men were dumbfounded. Where on earth could he have ever learned such perfect Yiddish?

After they paid their bill, they asked the restaurant manager, an old friend, "Where did our waiter learn such perfect Yiddish?"

The manager leaned toward them and said, "Shhhh! He thinks we're teaching him English."

A rabbi and a Catholic priest were discussing the future of the younger generation. The priest related that his nephew was attending a theological seminary in order to become a clergyman.

The rabbi inquired as to the ensuing career possibilities for the young student.

"Well," replied the priest, "he can become a chaplain."

"And then?" asked the rabbi.

"He could become a cardinal in time," answered the priest.

"And then?"

"Well, he might even become a pope."

"And then?"

The priest replied in amazement. "What more do you want? Do you imagine that he can become God?"

"Well," replied the rabbi softly, "one of our boys made it."

Sammy Cohen and his friend Michael Murphy had adjacent shops on New York's Lower East Side. After just five years, Sammy owns the whole block, while Michael still has only his small shop.

"Sammy, I'm fed up!" Michael said one day. "We both work the same. Tell me, what's the secret of Jewish business success?"

"Easy," replied Sammy, "gefilte fish."

"Gefilte fish? Well, could you let me have some?"

Sammy sells Michael a pound of gefilte fish for $10. On his way home, Michael noticed another shop selling gefilte fish for only $4 per pound. He returns to Sammy's. "Listen, Sammy, it's very kind of you to give me the secret of Jewish business success, but I saw gefilte fish for sale down the street at less than half the price."

"See?" said Sammy, "it's working already!"

*   *   *

A rabbi and a priest got into a car accident. It seems the priest had been tooling along at a rapid clip and smashed right into the rabbi.

Along came a cop, who looked the situation over quickly and then said in his thick Irish brogue, "Now, Father, tell me . . . How fast was the rabbi backing up when he hit you?"

Gold was in the middle of telling his friend a story: "One day, Cohen and Levine were going—"

"Cohen and Levine, Cohen and Levine," the friend stopped him angrily. "Why are your jokes always about Jews? Why don't you tell a joke about . . . oh, the Chinese for once?"

Gold was taken aback. "You're right," he said. "One day, Soo Lung Mu and Mao Tsu Nu were going to Soo Lung Mu's nephew's bar mitzvah. . . ."

A Jewish couple in Brooklyn won $20 million in the lottery. They immediately began living a life of luxury. They bought a luxurious mansion in Southampton and surrounded themselves with all the flagrant material wealth imaginable.

They decided to hire a butler, and to get the best, they flew to London. They soon found the perfect butler and brought him back to their mansion.

The next day they instructed the butler to set up the dining room table for four, explaining that they had invited the Cohens over for dinner, and that they would be going out for the day.

When the couple returned early that evening, they found the table set for eight. They asked the butler why eight when they specifically instructed him to set the table for four.

The butler replied, "The Cohens called and said that they were bringing the Bagels and the Bialys."

A rabbi had to spend time in a Catholic hospital. He became friends with one of the nurses, a nun. One day she came into his room and noticed that the crucifix on the wall was missing. She asked him good-naturedly, "Rabbi, what have you done with the crucifix?"

"Oh, sister," the rabbi said with a chuckle, "I just figured one suffering Jew in this room was enough."

Here are three Gentile jokes that Jews love to tell:

A Gentile goes into a clothing store and says: "This is a very fine jacket. How much is it?"

The salesman says: "Five hundred dollars."

The Gentile says, "OK, I'll take it."

A man calls his mother and says, "Mother, I know you're expecting me for dinner this evening, but something important has come up and I can't make it."

His mother says: "OK."

*   *   *

Two Gentiles meet on the street.

The first one says, "You own your own business, don't you? How's it doing?"

The other Gentile says, "Just great! Thanks for asking."

Three men of the cloth—a Catholic priest, a Baptist minister, and a rabbi—were counting collections taken during services for the week. They were trying to come up with an equitable way to divide the money between God (the two churches and one synagogue) and themselves (the clerics' weekly income).

The priest was the first to speak: "I know what! I'll draw a line down the middle of the sanctuary, toss the money up in the air, and whatever falls on the right side of the line is for God and whatever falls on the left side is for us."

The Baptist minister cried, "No! No! No! I'll draw a circle in the middle of the sanctuary, toss the money up in the air, and whatever falls inside the circle is for God and whatever falls outside the circle is for us."

The rabbi then asked the two other men to accompany him outside. There he offered this suggestion: "What I would do with the money is this: Toss it up in the air, and whatever God catches is His and whatever falls to the ground is ours."

What's the difference between a goy, an Ashkenazi Jew, and a Sephardic Jew?

The goy has a mistress and a wife and loves his mistress; the Ashkenazi Jew has a mistress and a wife and loves his wife; and the Sephardic Jew has a mistress and a wife and loves his mother.

For months, Mrs. Pitzel nagged her husband to accompany her to the Madame Freda's Séance Parlor. "Milty, she's a real gypsy, and she brings the voices of the dead from the other world. We all talk to them! Last week I talked with my mother, may she rest in peace. Milty, for twenty dollars you can talk to your *zayde* who you miss so much!"

Milton Pitzel finally could not resist her appeal. At the very next séance at Madam Freda's Séance Parlor, Milty sat under the colored light at the green table, holding hands with the person on each side. All were humming, "*Ommmmm, ommmmm, tonka tooom.*"

Madame Freda, her eyes lost in trance, was making passes over a crystal ball. "My medium . . . Vashtri," she called. "Come in. Who is that with you? Who? Mr. Pitzel? Milton Pitzel's *zayde*?"

Milty swallowed the lump in his throat and called out, "Grampa? Zayde?"

"Ah, Milteleh?" a thin voice quavered.

"Yes! Yes!" cried Milty. "This is your Milty! Zayde, are you happy in the other world?"

"Milteleh, I am in bliss. With your Bubbie together, we laugh, we sing. We gaze upon the shining face of the Lord!"

Milty asked a dozen more questions of his *zayde*, and each question was answered, until the voice said: "So now, Milteleh, I have to go. The angels are calling. Just one more question I can answer. Ask. Ask."

"Zayde," sighed Milty, "when did you learn to speak English?"

A man arrives at the gates of heaven. Saint Peter asks, "Religion?"

The man says, "Methodist." Saint Peter looks down his list, and says, "Go to room twenty-four, but be very quiet as you pass room eight."

Another man arrives at the gates of heaven.

"Religion?"

"Baptist."

"Go to room eighteen, but be very quiet as you pass room eight."

A third man arrives at the gates.

"Religion?"

"Jewish."

"Go to room eleven, but be very quiet as you pass room eight."

The man says, "I can understand there being different rooms for different religions, but why must I be quiet when I pass room eight?"

Saint Peter tells him, "Well the Catholics are in room eight, and they think they're the only ones here."

There was once a small Jewish population in an area that was dominated by Quakers. The Jews there had their own synagogue, and found their Quaker neighbors to be friendly. All in all, the two populations got on very well.

One summer there was a terrible fire and the synagogue was completely burned to the ground. The Jews were devastated, and began raising money to build a new synagogue. The Quakers quickly saw their plight and decided to lend a hand. They got together and had a meeting and decided that until the new synagogue could be built, the Jews should be able to pray in their meetinghouse on Friday nights and Saturdays, since they only needed it on Sundays. Furthermore, all funds placed in the charity box would go toward the rebuilding of the synagogue. The Jews of the community, and their rabbi, were overwhelmed by the generous offer—and so it was.

All through the time of the building, the Jews prayed in the Quaker meetinghouse on their Sabbath and the Quakers on theirs. As the months rolled by, the funds rolled in and the synagogue came closer and closer to completion. Finally, just before Rosh Hashanah, the synagogue was ready to be reopened. The rabbi decided that the first services would take place on Erev Rosh Hashanah, and he announced this at the services in the Quaker meetinghouse.

The whole community was outside the new synagogue for the grand festive reopening. Everyone was congratulating one another as the rabbi went into the synagogue, and walked up to the pulpit. He then had the Gabbai open the doors for his congregants to enter.

After a few minutes, the stream of people stopped, and the Gabbai went up to the pulpit to inform the rabbi that everyone had been seated and that the services could begin. The rabbi looked around and noticed something strange. He mentioned to the Gabbai that there seemed to be several, if not many, congregants missing. To this, the Gabbai replied: "I hate to tell you this, Rabbi, but you should know that some of your best Jews are Friends!"

On a Jewish holiday in Tokyo, Harry Ginsberg, far, far from his home in Staten Island, asked the Japanese hotel clerk, "Excuse me. Would you happen to know if there is a Jewish synagogue here in Tokyo?"

"Synagogue?" replied the clerk. "Ah so, Ginsberg-san. Ah yes! Is synagogue! Leave hotel, walk down street two blocks, turn left—*banzai!*—is synagogue!"

So Mr. Ginsberg left the hotel, followed the clerk's directions, and lo and behold, there was a synagogue. He entered. All of the worshipers were Japanese, as was the rabbi, and the Purim services had begun. Mr. Ginsberg happily joined in. When the services were over, he approached the rabbi and said, "My name is Ginsberg. I'm from America. I just want to tell you, Rabbi, how very happy I was to be with you tonight."

The Japanese rabbi beamed. "Is honor! But excuse, you Jewish?"

"Certainly," replied Mr. Ginsberg.

"That's funny," said the rabbi. "You don't look Jewish."

ABOUT THE AUTHOR

Bestselling author ALAN KING recently starred as the legendary Sam Goldwyn in the off-Broadway production *Mr. Goldwyn*. He lives in Long Island, New York.